C000006730

LNER LINES
IN THE
YORKSHIRE
RIDINGS

by

Peter Cookson & John E.Farline

ACKNOWLEDGEMENTS

Throughout the time during which this book has been compiled we have been very much aware of the debt of gratitude we owe to many people who have made a contribution in one way or another, both large and small. We mention here, by name, John Bateman of Leeds who made the whole of his collection of pictures available to us and helped with a number of matters of identification. Also we mention Bill Hudson who made a considerable contribution in various ways but, particularly, in the area of identification of rolling stock; the detail involved in some of the captions we owe directly to him.

Many other photographers have also been generous with their pictures and, where known, their names have been acknowledged; however, inevitably, there are some pictures that are anonymous but we express here our sincere thanks to all these photographers, known and unknown, whose work we have used. In the case of anonymous pictures the captions represent a best guess on our part and we have tried to make this clear in relevant cases.

Finally we place on record our indebtedness to the Railway Correspondence & Travel Society by virtue of our frequent resort to their monumental work *Locomotives of the* LNER and also, where appropriate, to Willie Yeadon's *Register of* LNER *Locomotives*. When the latter is complete, the two series of books will certainly be indispensable works of reference to all who embark on any book relating to LNER locomotives and their work.

P.C. & J.E.F.

This edition published by:
Book Law / Railbus Publications 2006
382 Carlton Hill
Nottingham
NG4 1JA

Copyright Challenger Publications, P. Cookson & J.E.Farline 1995
ISBN 1 899624 33 3
Printed by The Amadeus Press, Cleckheaton, BD19 4TQ
First published in the UK by Challenger Publications

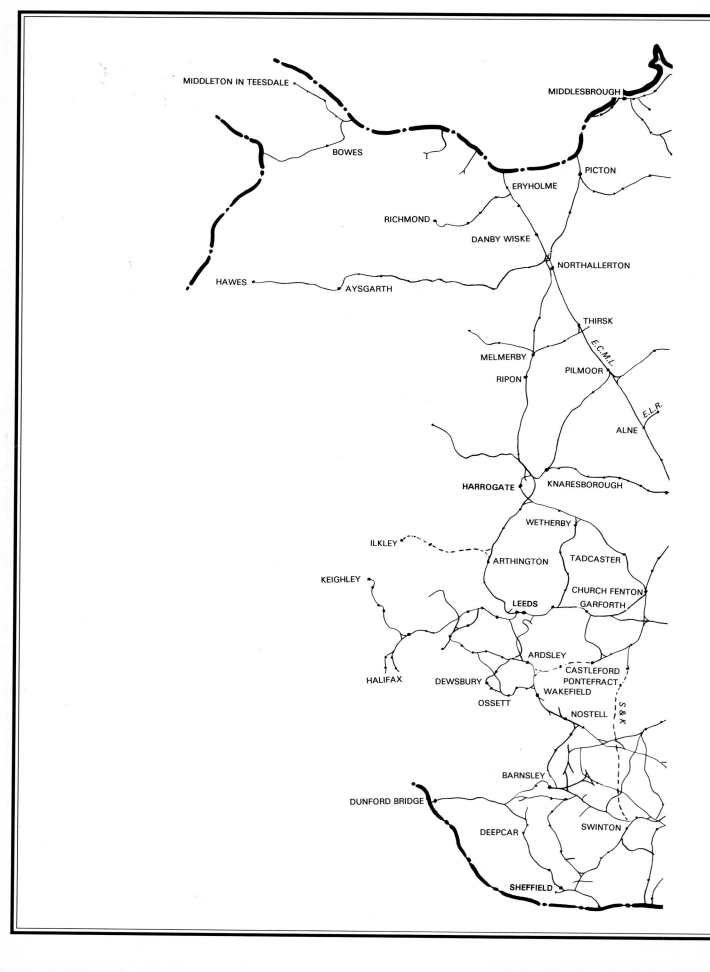

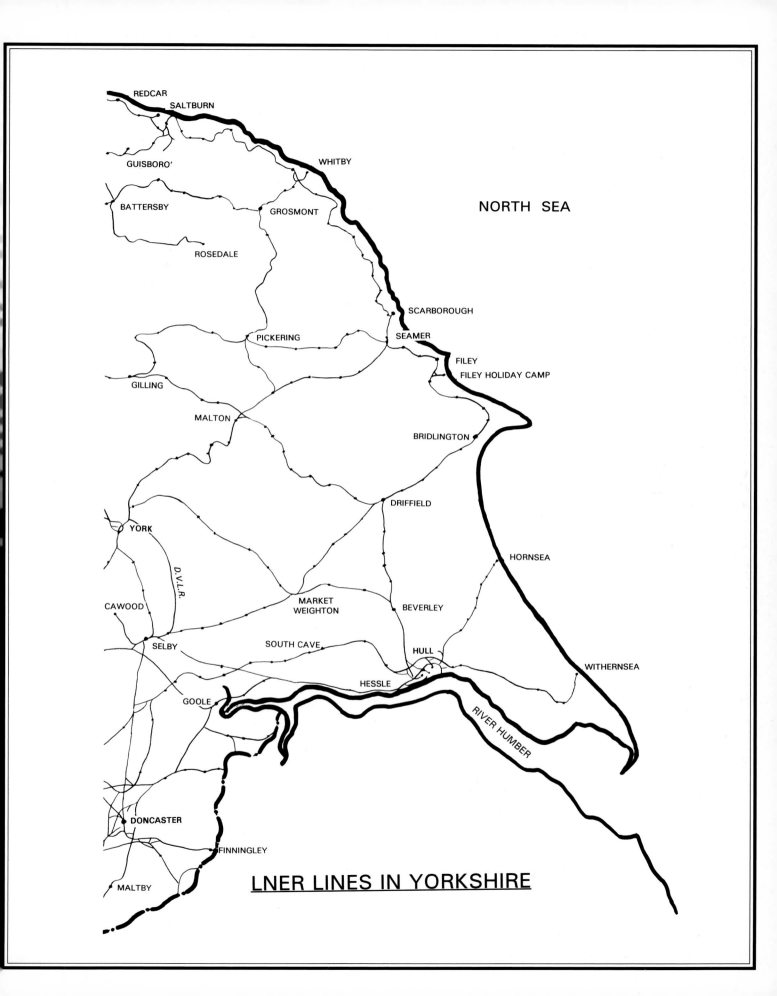

NORTH SEA

LNER LINES IN YORKSHIRE

INTRODUCTION

This book is not intended to be a history of the LNER Company, nor can it be exhaustive in its coverage of LNER lines in England's largest county. We have tried to put together a collection of photographs which show the variety of trains and scenes found on LNER lines before and after nationalisation within the boundaries of the old Ridings; with a smattering of pre-grouping views on the way. These range from industrial scenes to delightful scenic branch lines through the Yorkshire Wolds, Moors and Dales, the latter being unsurpassed by any other lines in the country for their scenic beauty.

The North and East Ridings were monopolised by the North Eastern Railway up to the grouping of 1923 and in some areas, particularly on the secondary and branch lines, right up to the introduction of diesels. The scene was virtually unchanged with NER locomotives, coaches, signals and buildings still in existence. In the West Riding the Great Northern and Great Central Railways predominated; the GNR mainly in the central area around Leeds and Bradford and the GCR to the south around Sheffield. However, even here the NER made incursions into the territory of the opposition with various joint lines and its lines to Leeds from York, Selby and Harrogate.

During the LNER years new designs of locomotives and rolling stock were introduced and these gradually spread throughout the system. One result of this was that pre-grouping express passenger locomotives which had been used on the East Coast Main Line were downgraded to secondary line use. An example of this was the ex-NER Atlantics which worked their final years on the Hull to Scarborough line.

Railway buildings remained generally the same as before 1923 so that to the casual observer nothing on the railways had changed and, as mentioned above, on the minor lines this situation continued well into nationalisation.

The photographs in the following pages have been grouped into four major areas centred on the cities of Leeds, York, Sheffield and Hull. Although we have tried to keep together those photographs which relate to places in a particular Riding, this has not always been possible. Examples of this are the scenes at Seamer Junction and Seamer Station; both locations were in the North Riding but the photographs have been included in the Hull and East Riding section. This is because the trains in both photographs were heading along the line from Seamer Junction to Hull, the bulk of which was in the East Riding.

Similarly, at Malton, the station was in the East Riding but most of the York to Scarborough line was in the North Riding. (The town of Malton was in the North Riding).

Steam power in Yorkshire survived nearly to the end of B.R. steam operations with the last working LNER locomotives being Class B1 4-6-0s. The Yorkshire Ridings disappeared as administrative areas in the boundary changes of 1974 when the pseudo county names of Humberside, Cleveland, West Yorkshire and South Yorkshire were created. Both West and South Yorkshire have since been removed from the administrative map and, as true Yorkshiremen, we look forward to the day when there might once again be three Ridings.

John. E. Farline., Wakefield.   *Peter Cookson., Pontefract.*

Class J26 0-6-0, No.525, comes off the York avoiding line and trundles past Holgate station as it heads towards Leeds and the west. The leading wagon is a five plank 10 ton, and this is followed by two eight plank 20 tonners, two eight plank 17 tonners, and then a mix of 17 and 20 ton vehicles. These types of mineral wagon were one of the trade marks of the North Eastern Railway and by Grouping over 17,000 of the 20 ton capacity had been built. The LNER continued to build wagons to the same design, but with detailed modifications. Being so numerous the wagons were seen far and wide and complete trains of gas coal ran from the Durham coalfield to East Anglia and Lancashire using these wagons. *W.Hudson collection*

Section One. **Leeds & The West Riding**

One could argue that Yorkshire's industrial West Riding had the most complex railway system in Britain, stemming from the physical and economic geography of the region. The former was basically an east facing slope from the Pennine watershed, down through wooded valleys and out onto the plains and marshes to the east. This slope was intersected by the west-east valleys of four major rivers - the Wharfe, Aire, Calder and Don. These rivers, together with innumerable fast flowing tributaries, of soft, lime-free water, provided ideal conditions for the establishment of fulling mills and domestic weaving. Underlying the area were vast deposits of coal and, in places, ironstone. The importance of these elements was dramatically increased in the late eighteenth century, when steam superseded water power and the Industrial Revolution began. Domestic industry moved into mills and factories, creating a demand for better transport facilities, housing and

commercial development. This progress in turn created employment which led to mass migration from the depressed agricultural south and east. Colliery villages and factory towns seemed to merge into one vast urban sprawl, although the rugged terrain and the Yorkshireman's individuality did not allow this process to finalise. It was indeed a region teeming with people and industry, but without a clearly defined regional centre. It was this presence of many towns and the rich rewards to be gained from the diverse industry that attracted the early railway promoters. Once established the companies strove to expand their empires by putting out tentacles in all directions. With ideal conditions the area continued to grow and, although we have said no one place seemed to form the regional centre, one place had a good claim to it - Leeds. It is here that we begin our brief tour of the LNER lines in Yorkshire.

The machinations which led to the opening of Leeds Central station can probably be considered as the most complex in the history of the West Riding railways. While the full story, so far as it is known, is beyond the scope of the present narrative, suffice it to say that the Great Northern Railway originally agreed to become a partner in building the station in 1846, gaining access to Leeds by running powers over the Midland Railway from Methley, obtained in 1847. A temporary terminus was opened at Central in September 1848, but such were the problems and disagreements that by 1850 there was a general exodus of the companies involved and in that year the GN opened a temporary terminus at low level, access to which involved reversal of all trains at Wortley Junction. The following year the London & North Western, Lancashire & Yorkshire and the Leeds & Thirsk railways agreed to become joint owners of and complete the construction of Central station. In 1854 the GN agreed to become a fourth partner, but it was not until 1857 that the station was completed. In November of that year the company began direct services into Central over the newly opened Bradford, Wakefield & Leeds Railway, and gave up its dependence on the MR for access. From that date the company and its successors were to run its principle services from London Kings Cross into the station for almost 110 years until it was closed on 1st May 1967, after all services had become concentrated on Leeds City station. Throughout this time Central was host to the prestige locomotives of the day, and in this view A4 Pacific 60008 DWIGHT D. EISENHOWER passes Leeds Central 'B' signal box with an up express in the mid 1950s. The Pacific was introduced in September 1937, as 4496 GOLDEN SHUTTLE, it was renamed on 25th September 1945, and received its BR number, 60008, in late October 1948. When photographed it still had its single chimney, but it was fitted with a double one during a casual heavy repair in September/October 1959. Unlike many of its sisters it did not face the cutter's torch and is today preserved at the Green Bay museum, Wisconsin, U.S.A. C.Marsh

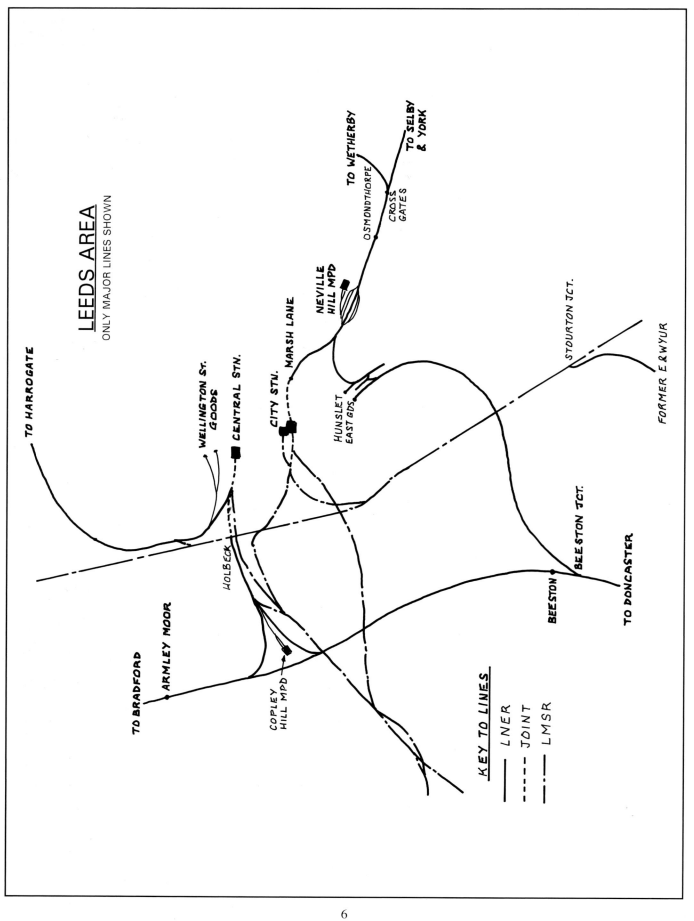

LEEDS AREA
ONLY MAJOR LINES SHOWN

TO HARROGATE

TO BRADFORD

ARMLEY MOOR

HOLBECK

COPLEY HILL MPD

WELLINGTON St. GOODS

CENTRAL STN.

CITY STN.

MARSH LANE

NEVILLE HILL MPD

OSMONDTHORPE

CROSS GATES

TO WETHERBY

TO SELBY & YORK

HUNSLET EAST GDS.

STOURTON JCT.

FORMER E&WYUR

BEESTON

BEESTON JCT.

TO DONCASTER

KEY TO LINES

———	LNER
– – –	JOINT
—·—·	LMSR

The spartan interior of Central station is seen here as one of the Copley Hill pilots, class J50 No.68988 removes two Pullman cars from the main arrival platform. These vehicles are, in fact, the Leeds portion of the down 'Queen of Scots' Pullman and are being removed for servicing and stabling in readiness for the next day's service. The introduction of Pullman services between London and Yorkshire had its origins on the Great Eastern Railway, which acquired an American General Manager, Mr - later Sir - Henry Thornton, in 1914. With much experience of Pullman travel Thornton saw no reason why Pullman services, then in use south of the Thames, should not prove popular in East Anglia. Accordingly an agreement was drawn up with the Pullman Car Company and various services began. While those on the Continental boat trains from Liverpool Street to Parkeston Quay became very popular, the remainder did not. When the LNER came into being in 1923 there was still a long period of the Pullman Car agreement to run and urgent consideration was given to finding a more profitable use for these vehicles. Apart from the Boat trains the remaining services were withdrawn and a set was made up to run between Kings Cross, Leeds, Harrogate and Newcastle, with the name 'Harrogate Pullman'. In 1925 the service was extended to Edinburgh and later the same year it was re-routed to run non-stop to Harrogate via Shaftholme Junction, Knottingley, Church Fenton and Tadcaster. This change preceded the introduction of a new train, the 'West Riding Pullman' (see page 12). There matters continued until 1928 when a new all-steel set of seven coaches appeared on the service, with the title 'Queen of Scots'. On the same date the 'West Riding' was moved to an afternoon departure from Kings Cross, and the 'Queen of Scots' returned to the Leeds route, leaving London at 11.15am. At the same time it was extended to Glasgow. Little further change took place, until withdrawal during the war, after which its popularity grew, such that by 1952-53 it had grown to a ten-car formation. The down train had a 3 hours 30 minutes schedule to Leeds, where eight of the cars were uncoupled and sent on to Glasgow. During the Beeching regime, when economies were the golden rule the service was curtailed at Harrogate, thus allowing one set of cars to make the return journey daily. As Scotland was no longer being served the title 'Queen of Scots' was dropped, and that of the White Rose' was transferred from its previous owner to the Pullman train. This was short lived however, for with the introduction in 1967 of high speed 'Deltic' hauled eight-coach trains the Pullman service was abandoned. *D.Pickersgill Collection*

The most likely motive power to be found on local services from Leeds (Central). This is N1 No.69485 polluting its dreary surroundings on the 26th September 1953 whilst awaiting its signal. *R.Copeman.*

Leeds Central in 1947 with the 'Yorkshire Pullman' departing for the capital behind A3 No.104 SOLARIO. The crew of B1 No.1196 take an interest in the proceedings whilst topping up their charge from the water crane. *W.B.Yeadon collection.*

While we have looked at the GNR services from Central station it must, of course, be remembered that the NER had a very strong presence in Leeds, with services north to Harrogate and eastwards to Hull, York, Scarborough and Newcastle. Originally a somewhat spasmodic service to the east ran from the Midland Railway's Wellington station via Methley, but increasing congestion at the former finally led the NER to deposit Bills, in 1864, for a direct line from Marsh Lane through the city centre to a new station north of Wellington Street. This would have involved such massive destruction of property that local opposition forced the company to abandon the proposal. A revised scheme, on a more southerly route, through some of the worst slums in Leeds, and through the graveyard of St.Peters church, was put forward the following year. (The line was to connect with a new station, to be built jointly by the LNWR and NER, on the south side of Wellington, and subject to rigorous conditions to prevent sacreligious noise and allow the reverent treatment of bodies, the line was approved.) The whole development was completed in 1869 when all LNWR and NER services were transferred to Leeds New station, leaving Central station to the GN and L&Y (although the LNWR continued to run one train annually into the station to preserve its share in the original agreement). Over the years the need for a single station in Leeds was raised from time to time, but it was not until 2nd May 1938 that Wellington and New stations were inter-connected and renamed Leeds City. Further pressure was applied but it was not until after nationalisation that a single passenger station was seen as an economic necessity. A £4.5 million scheme to concentrate all services on City station was put in hand in 1959, but was stopped in 1961 by a curtailment on capital expenditure. The scheme, now reduced in scope, was re-started in 1963. The work included major alteration of the track layout at Copley Hill junction so that traffic on the ex-GN route could gain access to City station. The work also involved the conversion of the former Wellington station into a parcels depot. The expanded City station and the new track layout was brought into use on 1st May 1967, on which day Central station was closed. Although Thomas Prosser's 'New' station had practically no frontage and added nothing to the architectural value of Leeds it did have a distinctive Mansard roof supported by very light trusses carried on foliated columns. At each end of the station were bay platforms for local trains, with traditional longitudinal canopies. These features are clearly seen in this view of 11th July 1949, as A3 Pacific 60086 GAINSBOROUGH stands at the eastern end of the station with an express for Newcastle. When photographed the engine was in pristine condition, having been in service less than two months since it had emerged from Doncaster works in the new pale blue livery.
D.Wilkinson/W.Hudson   collection

Few photographs truly capture the spirit of the steam age railway, but this evocative study of the prototype class G5 0-4-4T No.7240 (NER No.1096), at Leeds City on 20th January 1948, encapsulates the dim, smoky atmosphere of a large city station. The G5 tanks were introduced by Wilson Wordsell in 1894 and served for over 50 years with little alteration. Apart from moving the Westinghouse pump from inside the cab to the front of the left hand tank, the only other significant changes were modifications to the bunker to increase coal capacity. In 1917 a cage, with sloping sides, was fitted over the bunker and the rear spectacle plates were altered in shape. In 1921, three engines Nos.1096, 1884 and 1914 had coal rails fitted to the top of the cage. No.1096, along with 30 or so sister engines, was altered again following the introduction of mechanical coaling facilities, when a sheet iron hopper was fitted to the top of the cage to prevent spillage when being coaled. These engines put in sterling work on local passenger trains in Yorkshire and the North East, 7240 serving BR for nearly 10 years before withdrawal in April 1956. D.*Wilkinson*/W.H*udson collection*.

(*opposite*) Holbeck High Level station, seen in the background of this view as class A1 No.60141 ABBOTSFORD accelerates away from Leeds with the up 'Harrogate Sunday Pullman', marked the point where the GNR left the joint lines and assumed its own metals. The low level platforms, situated on the Midland route to Bradford and Skipton, were at right angles to the GNR platforms, and were added in 1862, seven years after the high level lines were constructed. The route out of Central station was quite steep and various catch-points were installed to deal with runaways. An interesting example can be seen on the left, where the blades would de-rail an offending vehicle, but a very long lead out would push them inwards, to prevent breaking through the parapet and crashing to the ground below. At first glance the train appears to be un-named, but a very grubby headboard is carried on the centre lamp iron. C.*Marsh*.

A3 60072 SUNSTAR is shown here during its brief five-month period of service working from Leeds Copley Hill shed in the summer of 1960, although its next move was only a very short one - accross the city to Holbeck. The angle of the sun and the headlamp code suggest the working is a late morning or early afternoon Leeds (Central) - Doncaster stopping train. The location is Holbeck (High Level) and Central terminus can just be seen in the centre background. The lines diverging to the left alongside the fourth coach of the train comprises the NER/GNR branch to Geldard junction. R.*Farrell.*

A1 Pacific No 60123 H.A.IVATT, of Ardsley shed, gets into its stride past Wortley South junction signal box with the up 'Yorkshire Pullman', in the late 1950s. Following the success of the Harrogate all-Pullman service introduced in 1923, the LNER sought to expand its activities in this field and the following year it introduced the 'Sheffield Pullman'. This ran from Kings Cross to Grantham and then via Nottingham Victoria to Sheffield Victoria, but it failed to attract custom. A month later it was re-named the 'Sheffield and Manchester Pullman' and was re-routed via Retford to Sheffield and Manchester Central. This too failed to attract significant patronage and in September 1925, following the revision to the 'Harrogate Pullman', the Sheffield set was used to form a new service to Leeds and Bradford. On arrival at Leeds two cars were detached and sent on to Bradford, while the Leeds portion was worked empty to Harrogate to form the 11.15 am to London, via Leeds, where the Bradford cars were picked up. From 1926 the Bradford portion was detached at Wakefield and its working was extended to Halifax. The arrangements were again altered in 1928. When the 'Queen of Scots' was put back on the Leeds route, the Harrogate set was renamed the 'West Riding Pullman' and its down departure time was changed from 11.10am to 4.45pm, thus giving Yorkshire passengers the benefit of two daily Pullman services. In 1935 it was decided to extend the service to Hull, the relevant portion being attached and detached at Doncaster. In view of this wider range of operation the train was renamed the 'Yorkshire Pullman'. In the autumn of 1937 the introduction of the 'West Riding Limited' streamliner service, with a mid-morning departure from Leeds, negated the need for a morning Pullman service from Bradford and Leeds. The Harrogate train was therefore diverted via York, before calling at Doncaster to pick up the two Hull cars, and the two which had been worked from Halifax via Bradford and Wakefield. Following reinstatement after the war, by which time it had returned to the Leeds route, various departure times were tried until in 1949, the train settled down to a 10.15am departure from Harrogate and a 5.30pm return from Kings Cross. The final changes to the service began with a cut in journey times following the introduction of 'Deltic' diesels, and the concession to Hull of its own Pullman service in 1967, which then allowed the 'Yorkshire Pullman' to run non-stop to Wakefield. The train continued to run until the end of the 1977/78 timetable, on a schedule of 2hr 55 min, but was then quietly forgotten. It has now been re-instated and runs today with Mk.4 coaching stock and electric Class 91 haulage. There are two sets of carriages, and such has been the acceleration of timings, that each set makes two return journeys daily between Leeds and Kings Cross. C.Marsh

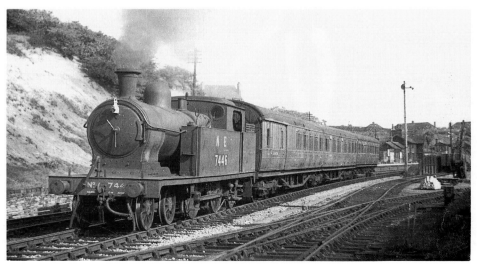

Former GC 4-4-2T, LNER class C14, No.7446, heads away from Beeston station into Leeds with a local train from Wakefield or Castleford, just after the war. The train is composed of a single pair of Gresley articulated stock (brake third and lavatory composite), with an eight compartment third at the rear. The C14s spent a long time in the West Riding, No.7446 being shedded at Ardsley when photographed, as clearly shown in traditional LNER style on the buffer beam. The engine was withdrawn at the end of 1956, by which time it had been transferred to Gorton.
P.Cookson collection

Another Leeds area local train of the same period, with ex GN class N1 0-6-2T No.9436, slowing for the Beeston stop with a Leeds - Castleford (Central) working. The train formation is exactly the same as the previous illustration, but the engine is too grubby to ascertain its depot, which would have been either Ardsley or Copley Hill. The N1s, perhaps more than any other type, were the typical motive power for LNER suburban services around Leeds and Bradford, until their withdrawal with the introduction of diesel multiple units in the mid 1950s. P.Cookson collection

Gresley A3 No.60052, PRINCE PALATINE, finds itself on a very humble duty working an evening Doncaster-Leeds local past Ardsley motive power depot, in the mid 1950s. It was not unusual to find this kind of working as Pacifics were often rostered for local trains as part of a more complex diagram. In the case of Doncaster-Leeds services they were also used as 'running-in' turns after overhaul at the 'Plant'. The most interesting element of the scene, however, is the train itself. The leading coach is an ex GC matchboard corridor third, in carmine and cream livery, behind which appears to be an ex LNWR brake third. At the rear is an unidentified eight compartment third. C.Marsh

The down 'Queen of Scots' Pullman races past Spring Lane, Ardsley with A1 No.60134 FOXHUNTER at the head. Completed in November 1948, this locomotive was withdrawn in October 1965, having spent much of its short working life at Copley Hill depot. The confusing array of signals is not as complex as might at first appear; the original wooden post, with its mixture of upper quadrant and somersault arms, was shortly to be replaced by a fabricated steel structure seen a couple of yards or so in front, but without arms. C.Marsh

A class J empty wagon train is seen in the vicinity of Tingley gas works, circa 1957, hauled by an unidentified Class O4 2-8-0 locomotive (probably from Ardsley shed) on the line from Adwalton Junction to Ardsley. The line seen curving in from the left is the branch from Batley (GN) through Woodkirk to Tingley. A.M.Ross.

(*above*) Reproduced from a copy of an old postcard, this picture of Stanley station, Methley Joint Railway, looking west towards Lofthouse Junction shows the attractive design of the main station buildings on the left; the steep angles of the hipped roofs are particularly noticeable. J.E.*Farline collection*

(*right*) Stanley signal box, situated on the opposite side of the main Wakefield - Aberford road from the station. Although the Methley Joint Railway involved the GN, NER and L&YR it was the first mentioned that had the principal interest and the stations and works along the line were of GN origin. The decorative barge-boards of the signal box are noteworthy as is the GNR somersault signal to the left with its spectacles about one third of the way down the signal post. J.E.*Farline collection*

A lovely period-piece photographed at Earlsheaton (near Dewsbury) some time before 1914. The locomotive crew and shunting staff pose proudly with their immaculate GNR Class L1 (LNER Class R1) 0-8-2T No.128 during shunting operations. These locomotives were originally a development of Ivatt's 0-8-0 mineral engine and intended for London suburban work but they proved to be too heavy and generally unsuitable, whereupon they were banished to the West Riding and Nottingham districts for freight working. No.128 was an Ardsley engine until it and its sisters were sent to join the others at Colwick early in 1914. J.E.*Farline collection*.

An unidentified B1 4-6-0 has just passed Earlsheaton station as it hurries a three coach formation of brake first, corridor composite and brake third, from Bradford to Wakefield, where they will be attached to a Leeds - King's Cross express. The original GN line from Wakefield to Bradford ran via Ossett and Batley, but the GN were keen to tap the lucrative traffic from Dewsbury, the centre of the heavy woollen industry. Consequently powers were obtained for a loop line from Runtlings Lane junction, west of Ossett, to serve Dewsbury. This was opened to a temporary station in the town in 1874, but this was a time of industrial depression and it was not until 1880 that a permanent station was opened and the loop to Batley completed. This line then became the principal route from Wakefield to Bradford and remained so until closure in 1965. The line passing through the gate on the extreme left served a colliery. A.M.Ross

Ex GNR 0-6-0 No.64268 (LNER Class J6), of Ardsley shed, approaches Runtlings Lane junction, a little under a mile east of Earlsheaton, with a short coal train in the late 1950s. The train is running from one of the many collieries in the Dewsbury/Batley area to Wrenthorpe yard, Wakefield and is probably returning the two leading brake vans to the yard to await their next turns of duty. The rather dilapidated single branch line climbing away to the right is the original line from Ossett to Batley via Chickenley Heath, opened in 1864; the line via Dewsbury (Central) was opened rather later in 1880 and assumed the greater importance for traffic between Wakefield and Bradford. In terms of physical geography the line abounded in severe gradients and many of the heavier trains - particularly longer excursion trains - had to be double-headed. A.*Robinson*

The Chickenley Heath branch, mentioned in the previous caption, is the setting for 'Ardsley tank', LNER class J50/2, No.68916, with a short mineral train in the early 1950s. The leading 12 ton wooden wagon is a former private owner wagon, still with pre 1923 round bottom grease axleboxes, but though it has traces of its original livery this is sadly indiscernible. The second wagon is also an ex private owner with 'cupboard' style side doors. In later years the branch was largely disused at the Runtlings Lane end but it was in regular use at the Batley end to service Shaw Cross Colliery until that pit closed about 1960. It was normal practice to work coal down to Batley yard in very short trains because of the severe gradients, as typified by this view of 68916 near Shaw Cross. A.M.*Ross*

A Leeds - Doncaster local train rolls into Wakefield Westgate behind class A2/2 No.60505 THANE OF FIFE. The A2/2's were Thompson's rebuild of the Gresley class P2 2-8-2's introduced in 1934 for the arduous Edinburgh - Aberdeen route. At nationalisation all six of the A2/2's were in service in Scotland but came south at the beginning of the 1950s, being equally divided between York and New England sheds. The train consists of a Thompson brake third and matching full third, followed by a Gresley composite and brake third. C.*Marsh*

The down 'Queen of Scots' Pullman comes off the '99 arches' viaduct and through the middle road at Wakefield Westgate behind A1 No.60120 KITTIWAKE, a type which dominated haulage of this train. By the time of this illustration, in the late 1950s, the original GN platform canopies, with their familiar saw-tooth barge boards, had been replaced by the featureless reinforced concrete design then in vogue. Today much of this scene remains, but the overall appearance has been greatly changed by the addition of overhead electrification wires and masts. A.*Robinson*

The Methley Joint line was an undertaking involving the GNR, NER and LYR, although the former had the major interest in it, and made the greatest use of it. The principal use of the system was the movement of coal, but for much of its life it did carry local services from Leeds (Central) and Wakefield (Westgate) to Castleford. It also enabled occasional excursion trains from Rothwell, on the East & West Yorkshire Union Railway, to run via Lofthouse Junction, Methley Joint Junction and Castleford to get to the east coast resorts of Scarborough or Bridlington. In latter years it also provided an ideal line for enthusiasts tours and this view shows one such Railway Correspondence & Travel Society special behind two class J6 0-6-0s. The leading engine, 64222 is from Ardsley shed, which normally provided motive power for workings in the area. E.E.Smith.

O2/4 No.63947 slogs up the slow line at Hemsworth with a train of South Kirkby coal, in an almost equal mix of wooden and all-steel mineral wagons, in September 1958. The three cylinder class O2 2-8-0's were Gresley's ultimate heavy freight locomotives and they saw a great deal of service on loose coupled coal trains such as this one. Visually they were handsome, well proportioned engines, but there was considerable variation within the class, depending on the type of boiler, cab or tender fitted. 63947, with 100A boiler, side-window cab and group standard 4200 gallon tender, makes a pleasant sight in the evening sunshine as she earns her keep in typical fashion. P.Cookson

Excursions to the east coast from points on the GNR system in West Yorkshire, such as Batley, Bradford, Ossett etc., which used the Methley Joint line to avoid Wakefield, were very often double-headed as far as Castleford, where the pilot would be detached. It was usual on summer evenings at weekends to find light engines waiting at Castleford for returning excursions in need of assistance over the heavy gradients on the final part of their journey. Such a sight is typified here with an Ardsley J6, still in LNER livery, and a named B1 in LNER apple green with BR number and lettering, standing on the Cutsyke branch just to the west of Castleford station. *D.Pickersgill collection*

A down Class H freight passes Castleford goods yard between the station and the level crossing signal box on 25th August 1960. The locomotive is Class B16/2 No.61435 - one of Gresley's 1937 rebuilds of the original Raven design. Both Gresley and Thompson produced modifications to the original locomotives, the latter being designated class B16/3. Although the rebuilds were very similar in appearance, they could be readily identified by the fact that the Gresley engines were right-hand drive, while the Thompson machines were left-hand drive. *P.Cookson*

A very grimy class Q6 0-8-0, No.63424, makes heavy weather of lifting a loaded coal train up the grade out of Kippax on the single line branch from Castleford to Garforth, about 1960. The branch was opened in 1878 as the Leeds, Castleford & Pontefract Junction Railway, but was worked from the outset by the NER. In the main it was a freight line, having been built to exploit collieries in the Kippax and Allerton Bywater areas, but until 1951 carried a Leeds City - Castleford local service. In this view the train is moving very slowly as the wind is carrying the smoke ahead of it! M.Baldwin

Thirty years ago the annual seaside holiday meant a journey by train for many, if not the majority, of holidaymakers and the next two views show such trains near Pontefract (Baghill) on the Swinton & Knottingley Joint line. With its connections to the Midland at Dearne Junction, the GCR system at Mexborough West Junction and the Barnsley - Manchester line via the Wath curve, the S&K Jt line was well placed to handle the heavy excursion traffic to the east coast via York or via Milford Junction and Selby. In this view a very clean Mexborough K3, 61868, with a train of ex LMS Period II and III stock, is seen just south of Pontefract on 30th August 1958. Although the reporting number is partially obscured by the vacuum hose, the train appears to be the Sheffield Victoria - Filey Holiday Camp train. Not only the use of the LMS stock is of interest, but the fact that four of the vehicles are still in carmine and cream a good two years after the 1956 livery changes. P.Cookson

Travelling south, in roughly the same location as the previous view, in the early afternoon is B16/1 No.61419, of Selby shed, with the Scarborough (Londesborough Road) - Leicester (Central) holiday train via the GC line. The hill behind the smoke is Bag Hill, from which the station took its name. The NER slotted past signal on the left is worthy of note. *P.Cookson*

One train which ran for many years over the S&K line and regularly brought Southern Region coaching stock to the north east was the Newcastle - Bournemouth through train, which ran via the GC route, Banbury and Oxford. This train is seen climbing out of the Aire valley, on 1st May 1958, and approaching Pontefract, the first stop from York, behind 61457 one of York's numerous B16/2s. These locomotives were regular performers over the line, on all types of trains from express passenger to local freight. *P.Cookson*.

The return working off the Brackenhill branch on Thursday 22nd May 1958, approaches Pontefract (S&K) from the south conveying coal from Hemsworth Colliery, ultimately, mainly bound for Gascoigne Wood yard, but initially to Pontefract (Baghill) for intermediate sorting. The locomotive (almost invariably at this time) is one of Selby's stud of Q6 0-8-0s no.63432. The Brackenhill branch, although designated a light railway, was in fact, able to take the largest freight locomotives and in its latter days (after the closure of Selby shed) was host to all kinds of freight locomotives - whatever appeared to be on hand at York shed suitable for the job. P.Cookson

Recently shopped Mexborough B1 No.61165, restarts a through goods from a temporary stop alongside Burton Salmon station in 1958. The NE splitting signal indicates that the train is bound for Ferrybridge and Pontefract, en route to Mexborough and Sheffield. On the passenger lines, to the left, the NE signals have been replaced by an LNER structure, which when photographed showed the road set for Castleford and Normanton. Both the station and junction have now disappeared from the scene, but four running lines remain and are still heavily used. P.Cookson

The north end of Church Fenton station on the 14th January 1949 with the Normanton line on the left and the Leeds line running through the centre of the station. Behind the camera is the main line to York whilst the lines branching off to the right went to Harrogate. The original (1847) station house stands just behind the structure topped by the water tower which incidentally was the pre-1904 signal box. Further to the right stands the erstwhile engine shed. Church Fenton north junction had just gone through a re-arrangement when this scene was captured and the neatness of the platelayers work is evident. J.Williamson collection.

D21 No.1245 skirts platform 2 at Church Fenton with a northbound train from Sheffield circa 1935. The D21 was, numerically, one of the smallest classes of 4-4-0 found on the LNER, there being only ten of them. All had been withdrawn before Nationalisation, 1245 was the last to go in February 1946. J.Hooper collection.

Hull Botanic Gardens B1 No.61215 WILLIAM HENTON CARVER, comes round the curve from Selby with an express for Leeds via Micklefield and Cross Gates. Selby engine shed (50C) and its coaling tower can be seen in the background with a J72 0-6-0T just visible. On the extreme left is a gated private siding serving what appears to be a coal yard. J.F.*Sedgwick*

Ex GC 2-8-0 No.63747, of LNER class O4/7 brings a class F express freight round the curve past the gasworks at Selby East junction, circa 1960. The O4's were introduced in 1911 and in 1939 thirty seven of them were rebuilt with a shortened O2 type boiler, but they retained a GC smokebox. These engines were normally used on heavy mineral trains and when photographed here 63747 could well have been deputising for the more usual mixed traffic locomotive. J.F.*Sedgwick*

Class B16/1 No.61440, drifts through Selby in 1958 with a summer extra returning from the Yorkshire coast. The train is a modeller's dream, with a BR Mk.I brake third at the head, followed by an ex GN composite. Behind these are five more panelled coaches, possibly ex GC and at least one more BR Mk.I. In the background, perched on the bridge itself, can be seen the control cabin for the swingbridge which spanned the River Ouse. The bridge was installed in 1891 just to the east of the original cast iron bascule structure which was built in 1840 by the Hull & Selby Railway. For many years the four tracks were gauntleted across the bridge, with the Down lines having their crossing vees at the north end and the point blades at the south end. By 1960 the gauntleting had been removed and replaced by spring and electrically operated points at the north end of the bridge. J.F.*Sedgwick*

Ivatt's numerically small class of mixed traffic 0-6-0's (LNER J2) were similar in appearance to the rather better known J6's but had larger wheels - 5ft 8ins as compared with 5ft 2ins - and this made them useful for passenger work. The photograph shows 3080 on a summer excursion passing through Selby station on the down through line, possibly bound for Bridlington during the 1930's. At this time 3080 was a West Riding locomotive and was based at Bradford (GN) for a number of years so has most likely worked through from Bradford, Leeds or Wakefield. R.*Copeman*.

An undated view of Selby engine shed probably in the 1930's showing N.E.R. freight locomotives of classes J27 and Q6, the nearest one being J27 No.1029 (later (6)5818). Although Selby had some responsibility for passenger workings of a local nature, the great majority of its work related to freight and much of this consisted of the working of coal trains from West Riding pits, for which these two classes of locomotive were eminently suitable; indeed, they were associated with the shed up to its demise in 1959. W.B.*Yeadon collection*.

Reference was made earlier to the working of the Yorkshire Pullman and this view shows the four-car Hull portion of the up train leaving Goole behind class V3 2-6-2T No.67684. When photographed, in the late 1950s, the train left Hull at 10.30 a.m., with the complete train going forward from Doncaster at 11.50 a.m. There was then a wait of a little over eight hours before the down train arrived, and it is most likely that the engine was rostered for a fill in turn, either to Hull and back, or possibly to Leeds. The V3 tanks were regular performers on this train, 67684 moving south from Middlesbrough to Hull (Botanic Gardens) in 1957. As it transpired they were to be among the final Gresley designs to remain in service. This particular engine was still at work at the end of 1964, by which time it had returned to the North East, where all nine of the remaining members of the class were allocated to Gateshead. In this view, just west of Goole station, the tracks to the right of the train lead to the dock area while the double track to the left is the former LYR branch to Pontefract, which also gave access to the NER Selby branch at Oakhill Junction. Observant readers, with appropriate interests, will note part of Goole Town football ground in the left background. A.M.*Ross*

One of the infrequent services operating in the Selby area was over the branch through Drax to Goole. This was a relatively short lived line being opened as late as 1912, by the North Eastern Railway, and closed during the 'Beeching era' in 1964. It was never extensively used but certain trains worked through from Goole to York for the benefit of commuters, and other traffic was generated by the Royal Army Ordnance Corps depot at Barlow. Daily passenger services over the branch were provided by a two coach auto-train, seen here at Goole, in the mid 50's behind class G5 0-4-4T No.67250 of Selby shed. This engine was one of 21 members of the class fitted for auto-working, and shared the working on the branch with sister engine 67273. Both were withdrawn as diesel multiple units took over such services, 67273 going in May 1957 with 67250 following some four months later.

A.L.Brown

Having travelled east from Leeds as far as the Goole area we can now look west and north of the city for the final part of section one. The original GNR terminus in Bradford was opened as Adolphus Street in 1855, but it was so badly sited that within a few months the directors of the then Leeds, Bradford & Halifax Junction Railway suggested that their trains should run into the Lancashire & Yorkshire Exchange station. Although plans were drawn up without delay it was not until 7th January 1867 that the ¾ mile link between Hammerton Street Jn. and Mill Lane Jn., on the L&Y Bradford - Low Moor line, was brought into use, and Adolphus Street station closed to passenger traffic. Through trains between Kings Cross and Bradford had been introduced by then and continued to run, albeit as through coaches only in later years, until the line between Bradford and Wakefield was closed in the mid 1960s. In this view during the closing years, begrimed B1 No.61022 SASSABY, with nameplates already removed, heads the Bradford portion of a London train past St.Dunstans signal box, Bradford, and through the platforms of the disused St.Dunstans station, which closed in September 1952. The track layout at this point was quite complex, with the lines in the background being the ex L&Y route to Halifax, while those behind the signal box comprise the ex GN route to Queensbury. The wagon in the background above St.Dunstans signal box is standing on the coal cells at Springmill Street yard, while the signal box just visible at the tail of the smoke is the ex L&Y box at Mill Lane Junction.

J.Bateman collection

B1 No.61016 INYALA passes Low Moor No.2 signal box, on the L&Y Bradford (Exchange) - Halifax route, with an express, probably bound for Manchester (Exchange). Seen here, sometime after 1959, when the electrification flashes were added to the running plate, this locomotive led a somewhat nomadic existence during its final years. In 1956 it was shedded at York, but was transferred to Neville Hill in 1957. It stayed there for several years, but had been sent to the ex-L&Y engine shed at Low Moor by 1964, from where it was withdrawn during the last week of October 1965. From behind the signal box in the right background a GNR branch ran to Dudley Hill, off which was a spur to a GNR goods depot situated some distance to the right. Neither of these could have attracted much traffic as they were closed as early as May 1933. J.Bateman collection

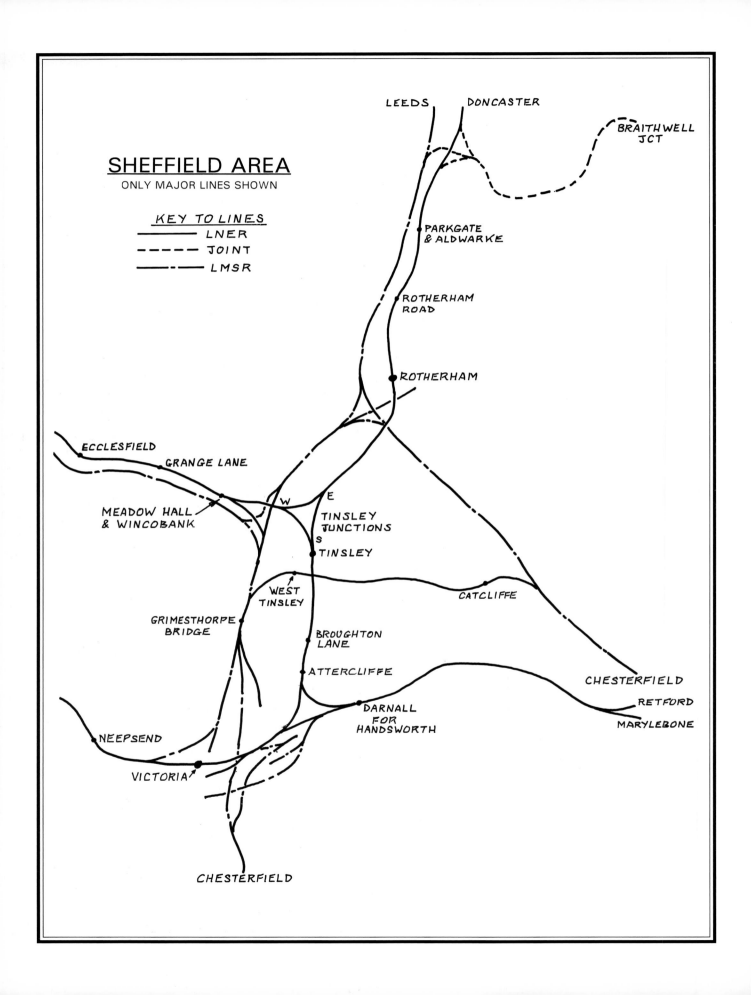

SHEFFIELD & SOUTH YORKSHIRE

Sheffield Victoria was the hub of the Great Central system in south Yorkshire, with passenger services radiating to Manchester, Bradford, Barnsley, York, Doncaster, Worksop and the east and Nottingham and the south. Apart from the Marylebone-Manchester expresses perhaps the best known passenger trains to use the station were the Harwich-Liverpool boat trains. For many years the class B17 4-6-0s (Sandringhams) were synonymous with these trains, working right through to Manchester in pre-war years. However, with the introduction of electric traction west of Sheffield, these engines came off at Victoria and were turned and serviced at Darnall shed before returning with the eastbound working. In this superb portrait, well groomed 61643 CHAMPION LODGE, of March shed, makes a spirited departure for Harwich, about 1955. D.*Pickersgill collection*

A through service between Bradford (Exchange), Huddersfield, Sheffield (Victoria) and London (Marylebone) ran during the GCR, LNER and BR eras, but it was not until May 1948 that the service was graced with the title "The South Yorkshireman". The up train is seen here, about 1953, pulling out of Sheffield (Victoria), behind a clean Gorton B1 No.61182 and heading for the Capital. The train would, most likely, have arrived in Sheffield from Bradford behind a former LMS Class 5 locomotive with engine-changing taking place at this point.

While the Sandringham's were regular performers on the boat trains they were not the sole performers, but of the substitutes a Stratford based 'Britannia' was most unusual. Although in a filthy state, the prototype of the class introduced in 1951, No.70000 BRITANNIA received much admiration from the enthusiasts as it drew away from Victoria, at some time during 1956. With the demise of the B17 class in the late 1950's, the 'Britannia' Pacific's took on this job on a daily basis until dieselisation saw them transferred away from the Great Eastern lines of the ER. N.*Stead collection*

LNER Class D10 (original "Director") 2657 SIR BERKLEY SHEFFIELD stands outside Darnall locomotive shed on 11th April 1948 in its short-lived 1946-48 numbering. Although in steam the engine wears a "Not to be moved, engine disabled" sign on the right-hand lamp-iron above the bufferbeam which suggests that the motion was being oiled by the driver. The plate also has the name W.Drinkle (drivers name?) at its centre so may well have been an early attempt of health and safety for staff on the railways. A*uthors collection*.

Wadsley Bridge station was situated a few miles west of Victoria on the Manchester line, in close proximity to Hillsborough football ground, which ensured that the station remained open after Victoria closed in 1970. On a day to day basis the station was served by local passenger trains, including a circular service from Penistone, Sheffield and Barnsley. Such a train is seen here entering the station on 19th June 1953 behind class C13 4-4-2T No.67434 of Barnsley shed. In contrast to today's two car d.m.u.'s, even such a mundane train was made up of four coaches comprising a Gresley eight compartment third, a Thompson brake third and third, and what appears to be a Gresley composite. At the rear are four horseboxes which are probably being worked home empty. B.R.*Goodlad*

The theme of the typical GC stopping train in the Sheffield area is continued in this view of the 4.45 p.m. Sheffield (Victoria) to Penistone local between Wadsley Bridge and Beeley woods, hauled by class C13 No.67424, on 19th September 1953. The locomotive is one of the Darnall (39B) contingent and is in quite good external condition with the lining on the tankside and footplate valancing clearly visible in the evening sunshine. Local services ceased on the line in 1959 with the closure of intermediate stations between Victoria and Penistone. B.R.*Goodlad.*

Main line trains on the Sheffield-Manchester section were primarily through trains between London and Manchester, and the Liverpool to Hull expresses. In addition to ex-GC classes, LNER A3s, V2s and B17s found work on the former trains at various times, but it was the Thompson B1s which became predominantly associated with them from about 1947 until they were turned over to electric traction in 1954. Climbing the bank up to Dunford Bridge, spotless B1 No.61159, of Gorton shed, with the 10.00 a.m. Marylebone-London Road is near Beeley woods, between Wadsley Bridge and Oughtibridge, on 17th March 1952. B.R.*Goodlad*.

For many years the heavy freight over the Sheffield-Manchester line was entrusted to the indigenous class O4 2-8-0s designed by J.G.Robinson of the GCR in 1911. These robust locomotives worked on such trains, without any serious rivals until ousted by the electrics, after which they were to be found on humbler duties. In this view class O4/6 (one of several variants of the original class) 63911 is on a down stopping freight near Oxspring in June 1958. A number of the original O4s were fitted with large boilers and these engines were classified O5 by the LNER. Subsequently rebuilt with standard type boilers, these engines were incorporated into class O4 as part 6. The shape of cab spectacle plates was a peculiar feature of the O4/6s. P.*Sunderland*

Penistone was effectively a railway crossroads, with ex GCR lines running westwards to Manchester via Woodhead, southwards to Sheffield and east to Barnsley and Doncaster. To the north was the ex LYR line to Denby Dale and Huddersfield, with the main station buildings located in the vee between the Manchester and Huddersfield lines. Penistone, with a population of just over 6,000 was a small, but important manufacturing and market town on the eastern slopes of the Pennines and the terminus of a number of local services. As far as the LNER was concerned stopping trains from Doncaster, Barnsley and Sheffield had Penistone as their destination. These trains were virtually monopolised by ex GC locomotives until withdrawal of services in 1959. Shown here is a typical service with class J11/1 0-6-0 No.64343, of Barnsley shed, leaving Penistone with a local train back to its home town. E.Blakey.

Approximately half way between Sheffield and Manchester lay the bleak uplands of Pikenaze Moor and Dearden Moss, which were originally pierced by the single bore of Woodhead tunnel, in December 1845. Even as this tunnel was being constructed it was envisaged that a second tunnel would eventually become necessary and twenty five side arches or refuges were built into the northerly side wall. Some two years later these were extended to form cross headings from which a second single bore tunnel was driven. Upon completion of this, in 1852, the tunnels became known as Woodhead Down Line and Woodhead Up Line respectively. Electrification of the line between Sheffield and Manchester was authorised by the LNER in 1936, using the 1500 volt DC system, with overhead conductors. Work had begun by 1939, but the outbreak of war brought an abrupt end to proceedings. When peace returned repair and maintenance of the tunnels resumed in preparation for electrification. The programme entailed the engineers taking possession of each tunnel for nine months, during which time single line working operated through the other tunnel. Quite why this work, with its associated disruption of traffic, was ever started, is something of a mystery, for not only was there a huge backlog of repair but the restricted bore of the tunnel prohibited the erection of the overhead catenary. It was therefore decided to build a new double track tunnel to modern clearances and this was authorised by the Railway Executive on 15th November 1948. The contract for its construction was awarded to Balfour Beatty and Co.Ltd. and work began in February 1949. During construction the original tunnels were of course still in use, and maintenance was still necessary. At such times the out of use line was marked by a flimsy tarpaulin barrier and a 15 m.p.h. speed limit was applied to the other line. These fixtures are seen on the left in this view, about 1950, as Gorton B1 No.61182 emerges from the Up tunnel with a Continental Boat Express. The leading coach is a Thompson corridor third still in teak livery, but the rest of the train is in the early BR 'Blood and Custard'. The appearance of the whole train reflects the fact that cleaning took a low priority as the railways struggled to regain their feet after the war. The new tunnel was completed in 1953 and opened to traffic on 14th June 1954, the day on which the Manchester to Penistone services went over to electric traction, and allowed through working of freight traffic from Wath, the Worsborough bank having been electrified on 4th February 1952. The section between Penistone and Sheffield Victoria was energised on 20th September 1954. J.E.F*arline collection.*

(*opposite*) As if in defiant mood, Class B1 No.61223 storms past Thurlstone signal box with a Marylebone-Manchester express on 10th May 1954, just a few weeks before steam gave way to electric traction. The signal box, sited just to the west of Penistone, is a standard GC type 5 box introduced in the late 1890s. This type of box can be recognised by the rather plain bargeboards, which did not have the central roundel found on the earlier MS&L type 2, 3 and 4 designs. B.K.B.G*reen*

In 1907 the GCR opened a new marshalling yard at Wath-on-Dearne, on the Barnsley-Doncaster line. It was the biggest such yard in Britain at the time and its purpose was the concentration of coal traffic from South Yorkshire, much of which went over the steeply graded Woodhead route to Lancashire. However the most fearsome gradient was not far from Wath and was encountered on the freight only line from Aldam Jnc. to West Silkstone Junction. Opened in 1880 by the construction of a connection from the original Aldham Jnc.-Moor End branch to a point west of Silkstone on the Barnsley-Penistone line, the line effectively by-passed the congested area of Barnsley. However the price of this 'by pass' was a gradient of 1 in 40 for 3$\frac{1}{2}$ miles in the vicinity of Worsborough. Much double-heading and banking of trains was necessary over such a line and the majority of the work fell to the native GC locomotives at Mexborough shed, but in this view the banker on duty was Gresley class O2/1 2-8-0, 63927. This was one of nine engines introduced in 1921 and was a development of an experimental Gresley GN 3-cylinder locomotive. The class was subsequently rebuilt with side-window cab and reduced boiler mountings. It is interesting to note that the tender, which is quite clean, appears to show no evidence of ownership, and it may well be that when photographed early in 1951, the tender was in process of having the insignia changed from LNER to BR, a job that was probably carried out by shed staff. J.E.*Farline collection*

This scene typifies industrial South Yorkshire and shows the view looking south at Mexborough South Junction, where the GC line from Sheffield to Doncaster passes between the River Don to the east and its Navigation Canal to the west. The grimy B1 and its train are unidentified, but the signals indicate that it is bound for Doncaster, and may well be one of the through trains which used to run between Liverpool Central and Hull via Sheffield Victoria. The lines to the left of the running lines gave access to Mexborough locomotive shed, which was situated to the east of the curve linking the South and East Junctions. A.M.*Ross*

The line from Doncaster to Barnsley was built by the South Yorkshire, Doncaster & Goole Railway (which became the South Yorkshire Railway & River Don Navigation) primarily to tap the rich reserves of coal around Barnsley, which could easily be sent to London via Doncaster and the Great Northern Railway. The first section of the line, from the MR at Swinton through Mexborough to Doncaster was opened in 1849. The following year a single line mineral railway was built from Mexborough to Elsecar, and in 1851 this was extended to Barnsley and doubled, after which passenger services were introduced. Eight years later the line was completed through to Penistone and passenger services were introduced between Penistone and Doncaster. They were to run for five months short of 100 years before withdrawal on 29th June 1959, when C13 No.67445 was captured at Wath on the last day of service. This engine was one of those displaced from Gorton, as referred to earlier, and although in run-down condition it has been decorated by some wag with two balloons, a wreath and a headboard. Professionally produced this reads 1857 - 1959 *Penistone Doncaster*. A *Century's progress and now this* - RIP. A pity the original date is two years too early! One wonders if the same wag made up the train for surely a Gresley seven compartment First and Thompson six compartment Third cannot be considered a typical local passenger train on such a route. N.*Stead collection*

Stairfoot, in the eastern suburbs of Barnsley was at the convergence of a number of GC routes together with a spur from the Hull & Barnsley Railway at Cudworth. The station also served Ardsley (not to be confused with Ardsley near Wakefield) and the station nameboard indicates this as can be seen to the right of the locomotives, though it is looking rather the worse for wear with the F of Stairfoot having almost dropped off! The train is one of a number of Pullman Specials which ran during the 1950s under the name of *Ian Allan Trains Illustrated Excursion* and the motive power is provided by two nicely turned out Class D11 (Directors) 62664 PRINCESS MARY and 62662 PRINCE OF WALES. A.L.*Brown*

(*opposite*) Barnsley, like Sheffield and Wakefield, suffered from George Stephenson's policy when building the North Midland Railway, of adhering to maximum gradients at the expense of by-passing important towns. As a result Barnsley's 'main line' station lay 3 miles north east of the town centre, at Cudworth. For thirty years this meant a road journey, but in 1870 a branch was opened from Cudworth South Junction to Barnsley Court House. Although the latter was jointly owned by the MR and MS&LR, it was the Midland and its successors which worked the passenger services to Cudworth, almost up to their withdrawal in June 1958. However, for a short time from 1957, displaced C14 class 4-4-2Ts from Gorton shed were sent to Barnsley to eke out their final days on local trains in that area. One such service was that to Cudworth headed by 67448, with painted 36D on the smokebox door, standing in platform 3 at Cudworth on a dismal day in June 1957. The train consists of a Stanier nine compartment non-corridor third and a six compartment brake. *J.F.Sedgwick*

(*opposite bottom*) During the preparation of the Act for the proposed Midland line from Cudworth to Barnsley it was agreed that the station planned for Barnsley would become the joint property of the MR and the MS&L. Before this the MS&L had used the 'bottom' station, but the general state of the station and the curving, 1 in 50 start on the Penistone line (opened throughout on 1st December 1859) were far from ideal. When the MR line opened in May 1870 a temporary station was brought into use, but during 1871/72 the adjoining Barnsley Court House was adapted to form a station and the name was retained. The station had a lightweight overall roof, with wooden platforms below and timber screen walls either side. The principal services using Court House were all local trains, either Sheffield-Barnsley or Doncaster-Penistone, one of which is seen in the mid 1950s behind class C13 4-4-2T 67434. On the left stands the driving trailer of the Barnsley-Cudworth push-pull unit, the other regular service from the station. *N.E.Stead collection*

(*below*) A superb overall view of Barnsley engine shed and Exchange station, together with Jumble Lane crossing and its associated signal box. The line from the Midland Railway at Wincobank & Meadow Hall to the Manchester and Leeds Railway at Horbury was opened in stages between 1850 and 1854, with the section north of Barnsley opening first. Prior to the opening it had been agreed that the line should be leased to the M&L, while the southern portion was worked, when opened, by the South Yorkshire Railway. This eventually led to the unusual situation of an end-on junction in the centre of the station (which carried the suffix Exchange between 1st August 1924 and the closure of the adjoining MR Court House station in 1960) between the L&Y and GC. The most unusual aspect of Exchange was that it only had one platform, a feature which the authors cannot readily explain. It was almost certainly not a question of lack of space for in the 1850s the town was quite small; nor was it the proximity of the engine shed. The original locomotive facilities consisted of a single road shed north of the station, near Old Mill Lane bridge. The depot seen here was built much later by the GCR, whose locomotive designs always dominated the allocation. Being a freight depot the engines on view are mainly 0-6-0 and 2-8-0 tender types, with three class C13 4-4-2 tank engines, 67447 nearest the camera, used for passenger workings to Penistone, Doncaster and Sheffield. The signal box is so nondescript as to defy classification and may well be the original box built by the South Yorkshire Railway, although the flat roof is a modern feature. Barnsley shed was closed on 4th January 1960 and the site cleared. Opportunity was then taken to add a second platform to the station and a footbridge. *P.Cookson collection*

Space was always a problem at Barnsley, for the land fell away quite steeply just north of the shed, and it was normal practice at weekends to stable locomotives some distance from the shed, south of the Midland route into Court House. Such a scene is depicted on Sunday 19th May 1957, with ex GC 2-8-0s dominant. On the right is class O4/8, No63731, which has obviously been subject to a bit of rough shunting. Part 8 of class O4 was a Thompson rebuild using the chassis of the O4, but incorporating a new standard 100A boiler and a new design of side-window cab. On the left stands 63913 of class O4/6; this engine was one of eleven rebuilt from class O5 in 1924. W.Potter

Like Barnsley, Mexborough engine shed was primarily a freight depot and this 1947 view shows one of the usual inhabitants, ex GC class J11/3 0-6-0, No.4442. This class was a Thompson rebuild of the original Robinson design, using piston valves and incorporating shorter boiler mountings. As such they came to be regarded as a standard class under Thompson's rationalisation of locomotive classes in the early 1940s. Behind 4442 can be seen one of the huge S1/3 0-8-4 tank engines, 9905, used for hump shunting in Wath yard. The original 3-cylinder locomotives had been built by J.G.Robinson in 1907 for this specific duty, but 9905 was rebuilt by Gresley in 1932 with various refinements to the original design including side window cab and sloping side tanks to improve forward vision. At the same time boosters were fitted to the trailing bogie to enhance power on the very arduous task for which they were designed, but the boosters were later removed. *Lance Brown*

Doncaster was an important crossing point of the river Don in Roman times, and from the medieval period it developed as a commercial and trading centre. By the early nineteenth century it had become famous for horse racing and with such an aristocratic image the townsfolk were not in favour of the railways, seeing them as 'unnecessary and uncalled for'. It was, in fact, not until 1849 that the Great Northern entered the town from the south, with a temporary station, replaced by a more permanent structure the following year. Its establishment as a 'railway town' came in 1853 when the company's locomotive, carriage and wagon works, known as the "Plant", were brought into use. The original station was considerably rebuilt and enlarged between 1873 and 1877 and almost since then it has been a mecca for railway enthusiasts. One of the main vantage points was the long island platform on the west side of the station, which gave an uninterrupted view of the main through lines. In this view, on 26th March 1948, with the scene dominated by the long footbridge giving access to the Plant, A4 Pacific No.30 GOLDEN FLEECE, comes through with an up express, while B1 1064 awaits departure with an up local. *D.Wilkinson/W.Hudson collection*

A general view of the south end of Doncaster station from an old pre-1914 postcard. The picture abounds in interest; on the left, standing at the buffer stops, is one of the small class of Ivatt 4-2-2s built for fast, light express work between 1898 and 1901; less well known than their illustrious forebears, the Stirling Singles, but evidently good performers apart from rough riding at times; the locomotive appears to be No.267. In the centre is G.N. saddletank, No.1241 engaged in shunting a four-wheeled coach. On the right, waiting in the engine lay-by near the end of the main up platform is No.1371, one of Ivatt's 4-4-0 passenger engines of 1900-2 (class D3/4). The long footbridge crossing the whole picture gave access to the 'Plant' works and, at the time of the photograph, midday, was crowded with workers. The second vehicle from the left appears to be a mail coach with its bag catching net extended. *D.B.Woodward collection*

Trains from the Great Eastern section of the LNER reached Doncaster by means of the GN&GE joint line from March via Lincoln. Such trains were eagerly awaited by enthusiasts in the 1950s as they may have produced ex GE class B12s or D16s as motive power. Most trains from this section, if not terminating, would change engines, and this view shows D16/3 No.62571, having arrived from the south and uncoupled from its train, running tender first on the up through line, to Doncaster Carr locomotive shed for servicing. This particular engine was fitted with the Whittaker tablet exchange apparatus near the bottom of the leading edge of the tender side sheet. This mechanism was fitted to a number of locomotives working on the mainly single track Midland & Great Northern system. *M.Crawley*

The new order. To the west of platform 8 on Doncaster station lay the Plant sidings and the goods lines, here occupied by a very grimy class J39 0-6-0, 64909, of Doncaster shed, with a permanent way train. However there is no interest whatsoever in what was then a workaday scene, for all eyes are on the prototype 3,300 hp Co-Co diesel locomotive, Deltic. It was in December 1954 that English Electric decided to invest in the construction of this locomotive, after successful use of the Napier-Deltic diesel engine in marine applications. Although it was conceived as a powerful express locomotive to meet BR needs, its export potential was borne strongly in mind. Hence its overall design and its striking blue and yellow livery, with a dummy headlight at each end, was very much North American in style. Its construction was completed in October 1955 and it began trial working on the west coast main line from Speke Junction. With electrification approaching the locomotive's future lay elsewhere and in January 1956 it was transferred to York. After a couple of minor mishaps due to its being slightly out of gauge it was transferred to Hornsey towards the end of the month, but it failed on arrival and was sent back to works for a replacement no.1 power unit. Once back in service it found regular employment on main line duties where its success resulted in BR placing an order for 22 similar machines in 1958 to replace 55 Pacifics. After failing at Doncaster in 1961 Deltic was returned to English Electric's Vulcan Foundry, where, after many abortive attempts at export sales, it was restored and finally presented to the Science Museum in Kensington. *A.Robinson*

It was normal practice to stable a stand-by engine in a siding to the south of Doncaster station in the event of a main line failure. It was usually a duty for a Pacific locomotive and on this particular occasion the engine is A2/3 class 60523 SUN CASTLE a member of Doncaster's Pacific stud at the time. The photograph was taken on 8th September 1960 from the window of a Norwich - York train as it slowed for the station stop. In the writers' experience the stand-by locomotive provided at the north end of the station in the late 1940s was usually one of the surviving GN Atlantics, so it was evidently not regarded as necessary to provide emergency Pacific power to Leeds or York. M.R.*Lake*

The locomotive shed in Doncaster was a large depot situated some distance south of the station, on the up side of the main line in the area known as the Carr (or Carrs), and was often referred to by this name. It had a large allocation of locomotives to cover all types of work from express passenger to yard shunting. With such a range of duties and an emphasis on top link passenger work, it is not surprising that the shed was one of the first to receive mechanical coaling facilities when the LNER embarked on its modernisation programme in the late 1920s. In this view the tower is host to Gresley A1 (later A3) class 2543 MELTON, in the original LNER apple green livery, with insignia on the tender side, and this helps us to date the view. In 1928 the decision was taken to move the engine number from the tender to the cabside and to move down and enlarge the letters LNER. It is known that 2543 received a heavy repair between February and June 1928, at which time it would have been repainted. Having been so treated it would have been scheduled to receive new insignia on its next visit to the works, which transpired to be a General repair between 17th April and 1st June 1929. Having lost a little of its ex-works sheen, and judging by the weathering of the coaling tower, one would date the illustration as early 1929. M.*Crawley collection*

THE PLANT

As mentioned earlier, the locomotive works of the Great Northern Railway were established in Doncaster in 1853, before which they had enjoyed a brief existence in Boston. This was simply because the complex railway politics of the late 1840s resulted in the first section of the GNR to be opened being that between Peterborough and Lincoln, of which Boston was roughly the geographical centre. However, as the system grew, Doncaster became much more important and the move was made. With the transfer of 900 workmen and their families, and subsequent growth, the population of the town increased from a little over 12,000 to 16,406 between 1851 and 1861. In the early years of the GNR, new locomotives were built by outside contractors, a common practice at the time, but in 1865-6 substantial extensions to the works were made and the building of new engines began following the appointment of Patrick Stirling as Chief Mechanical Engineer. A new erecting shop was built in 1890-1, a new carriage shop seven years later, and new repair shops in 1900-1. By this time the combined works area covered 200 acres and employed 4,500 men. For almost a hundred years the works, always known as the 'Plant', turned out some of the most famous and graceful of all steam locomotives. The Plant gates in Hexthorpe became an irresistible magnet for enthusiasts straining to see which locomotives were visible in the works and the following views have been selected to show typical examples in the Plant yard.

Single-chimney A4 No.60003 ANDREW K.McCOSH being steamed after emerging from repair in the blue livery adopted for top link locomotives. The shade was generally referred to as Caledonian blue, but the instability of the pigments rendered it an unwise choice in a regime which was to demand repainting only after general overhauls. It was therefore subsequently decided to abandon the blue livery, applied on the ER to A1, A3 A4 and W1 classes, repainting these engines in the standard Brunswick green for express passenger locomotives. In passing it is interesting to note that the livery on 60003 is not quite correct as the nameplate should have a black background. *M.Crawley*

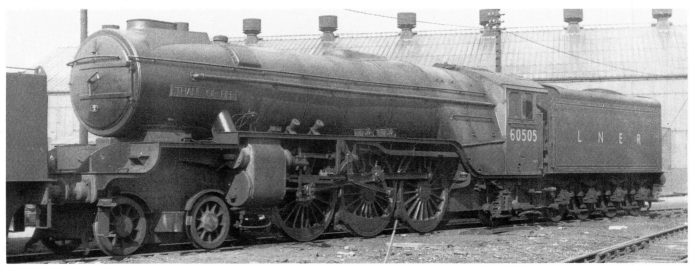

Class A2/2 Pacific, 60505, still basically in LNER green livery, on the stripping road outside Crimpsall shop on 26th April 1950. Having received only its BR number and shedplate it has obviously not undergone major repair for some time and on this occasion has come into works for a 'General'. It emerged on 13th June in lined Brunswick green. *M.Crawley*

Seen outside the weigh house on 23rd March 1950, class N1 0-6-2T, 69448 of Bradford shed, is fresh from the paint shop. It is in the standard 1949 intermediate livery of gloss black, lined in red, cream and grey. It has, however, been incorrectly given a black buffer beam, which should be painted vermilion. M.*Crawley*

We leave our brief visit to the Plant with a view of what at first appears to be one of the works shunters, but it is actually one of New England shed's class J52 0-6-0ST's No.8880. Although a BR shed plate has been fitted the engine is still in LNER condition and has probably come in for a long awaited 'general' repair. M.*Crawley*

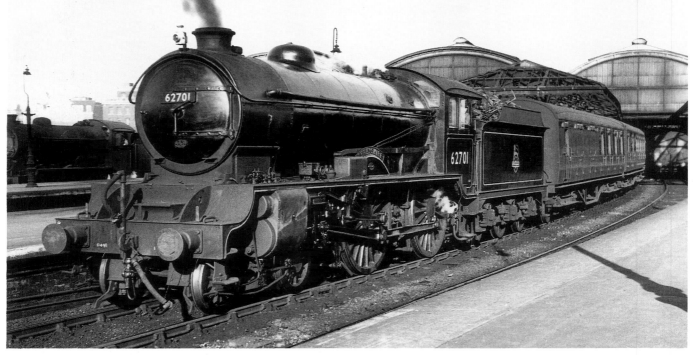

Coupled to an ex-GCR tender, a clean D49/1, 62701 DERBYSHIRE, of Bridlington shed (53D), awaits departure from Hull Paragon with a stopping passenger train. Paragon, opened in 1848, was the second station in Hull, replacing the original Hull & Selby station which was situated in the dock area adjacent to the River Humber. It equalled York as the second largest station owned by the NER, the largest being Newcastle Central. N.E.S*tead*.

A7 69781 of Dairycoates shed comes off the bridge over Anlaby Road, Hull with a lightweight train of vans heading to Neptune Street goods station. In the left background Anlaby Road Junction box can just be seen. At the junction the line to the left continued through Botanic Gardens and Wilmington in a curve around the city until it eventually reached the docks area. The line to the right carried on to West Parade Junction and Hull Paragon station. The shunting signal on the right appears to be a Hull & Barnsley example although the location is on an ex-North Eastern line. J.F.O*xley*

A collection of ex-NER 0-6-0 tank engines await their next turn of duty at Alexandra Dock, Hull. This was the site of the Hull & Barnsley two road wooden engine shed built in the 1880s. By 1913 it was decided that it was beyond repair and should be replaced. However, this did not happen and it remained in use until December 1927. Demolition then took place but a replacement shed was never provided with the result that engines had to stand out in the open air. On 27th October 1963, Alexandra Dock's allocation of locomotives was transferred to Dairycoates although the old shed area was retained as a signing-on point. R.J.*Buckley*

Class Y8 0-4-0T Nos.563 and 560 stand inside Hull Dairycoates shed during 1931. This was the largest locomotive depot on the North Eastern Railway and the engines were two of the smallest to work on the LNER. Designed by T.W.Worsdell as NER Class K, they weighed $15\frac{1}{2}$ tons and had a tractive effort of 6,000 lbs. They were introduced in 1890 and the last one was withdrawn in 1956. *Locofotos.*

One of Robinson's "Large Director" 4-4-0s, LNER class D11/1 No.2665 MONS, heads a Hull-Sheffield (Victoria) express near Ferriby in 1947. The locomotive is carrying its 1946 number which it would have borne for only two or three years before renumbering in the British Railways fleet. A.L.Brown

A stopping train for Hull leaves Withernsea behind L1 67754 of Botanic Gardens shed about 1955. Note the unusual design of NER bracket signal on the left. The station layout was also unusual as there was a turntable at the end of the line behind the train. The Hull & Holderness Railway was built as an independent line and was one of the few in the North East which had its own locomotives and coaches. Opened on 28th June 1854, the H&HR worked the line up to the end of 1859 when the NER took over working of the line. Authority for amalgamation was given on 7th July 1862. J.F.Oxley

An express hauled by one of Thompson's L1 2-6-4 tanks, 67766, rushes through Swine station on the line from Hull Paragon to Hornsea. The staggered platform arrangement, one each side of the level crossing, was a fairly common feature on some of the East Riding branch lines. The Hull & Hornsea Railway commenced life as an independent company on 28th March 1864. Trains from Hornsea ran into a terminus at Wilmington but by 1st July 1864 they were able to continue on to Paragon. The railway was formally taken over by the NER under an act of 16th July 1866; having, in fact, worked the line from the outset. J.F.Oxley

A5/2 4-6-2T 69836 of Botanic Gardens awaits departure from Hornsea Town with a train for Hull Paragon. The station building in the background was designed by Rawlins Gould of York who had been an employee of the Y&NMR architect G.T.Andrews. It is, therefore, not surprising that the station architecture on the Hull to Hornsea line shows similarities to that employed by Andrews on the smaller East Riding stations of the Y&NMR. The portico at Hornsea was very similar to that designed by Andrews for Whitby station. J.F.Oxley

Another Botanic Gardens engine, G5 67337, awaits departure from Little Weighton with a stopping train from Hull to South Howden about 1955. Designed by Wilson Wordsell and introduced as NER class 'O', 110 G5 0-4-4 tank engines were built at Darlington. No less than 51 of these sturdy little machines were still in service in 1956, seven of which were allocated to Botanic Gardens. The train, which would appear to have been strengthened above its normal length consists of a Thompson four compartment brake third, a lavatory brake composite, a Thompson full third and an ex NER full third. J.F.Oxley

An unusually clean class WD 2-8-0, No90094, of Hull Springhead shed, passes Little Weighton signalbox with a heavy train of coal from the West Riding, on 23 April 1955. Designed by R.A.Riddles for the Ministry of Supply these locomotives were introduced in 1943. Of the 733 built, 200 passed into LNER ownership after the war as class 07. They were scattered far and wide from Dundee to March but interestingly at the end of the LNER none were shedded in the Hull area. The train itself consists primarily of various designs of 16 ton all-steel mineral wagons, but there is a rake of six 12 ton wooden wagons near the head of the train. Three of these carry traces of private owner livery and while this is not legible one has lettering whose shape, style and spacing is very close to that of Clay Cross Colliery Company. J.F.Oxley

Push-pull fitted G5 67282 stands with its train of ex-NER coaches at South Howden station on the ex-H&B line before setting off for Hull on a misty day in the mid 1950s. Howden was the largest settlement served by the H&B between Hull and the South Yorkshire coalfield and the station was much closer to the centre of the town than the competing NER station. J.F.Oxley.

As the Hull & Selby Railway occupied the strategic route along the banks of the River Humber the Hull and Barnsley had no choice but to climb over and through the Yorkshire Wolds. In so doing it had to drive three tunnels, Drewton in the east, Sugar Loaf, and Weedley. Sugar Loaf, seen here on 28 March 1955, as class G5 No67282 emerges with a west bound push-pull train, was by far the shortest at 132 yards in length, but its construction nevertheless left a huge chalk scar on the hillside. At this point the line falls steeply towards South Cave and catch points were installed to deal with any breakaways to the heavy mineral trains using the route. J.F.Oxley

A post nationalisation scene which had remained virtually unchanged from pre-grouping days. Class A8 4-6-2T 69890 passes Cherry Tree signal box, Beverley, with a Hull to Scarborough stopping train. The signalbox is the NER Southern Division type and behind the engine a NER slotted timber post lower quadrant distant signal can just be seen. The A8s were usually used on the Scarborough to Whitby and Middlesbrough services but, occasionally, they were given a run down to Hull and back. It was common practice on the Hull to Scarborough line for one or two fish vans to be coupled between the locomotive and the first carriage, in this case an ex-NER clerestory, and anyone travelling in this vehicle would have been well aware of the van's contents! C.T.Goode

B16/1 61469 takes a homeward bound 'Saturdays only' extra through Driffield station circa 1956. The train is signalled for the line to Market Weighton. Originally the station had an all over roof but this was removed in 1949. On the left the small signalbox, named Driffield Station Gates, was used for control of the level crossing as the main signalbox at Driffield was located further south at the junction of the lines to Hull and Market Weighton. J.F.Sedgwick

B1 61377 approaches Wansford Box at the north end of Driffield station on its way to the coast with a trainload of holidaymakers. In the left background is Driffield goods warehouse which was designed by the Y&NMR architect G.T.Andrews. Other Andrews buildings, with their typical wide overhanging eaves, can be seen on the right and behind the coaches at the rear of the train. A.M.Ross.

A year before the final closure of the Malton to Driffield line in 1958, class J27 0-6-0 No.65849 of Malton shed (50F) shunts the twice weekly pick-up goods at Sledmere & Fimber station. The passenger service had been withdrawn in 1950 although it was occasionally re-instated during periods of heavy snow to provide transport for stranded villagers. A.M.Ross

A view at the south east of Sledmere & Fimber station looking towards Malton. J27 No.65849 waits for the manual crossing gates to be opened before proceeding across the B1248 Beverley to Malton road. The sign on the cottage on the left states that this is Fimber Road. As can be seen, the road crossed the railway at a very acute angle with the result that the gates at each side of the crossing were a considerable distance apart. A.M.*Ross*

A J27 0-6-0 passes the disused chalk quarry at Burdale, between Wharram and Sledmere, just after leaving Burdale tunnel. The tunnel was just under a mile in length. The buildings along the line, including the cottage in the left background, used bricks which had the letters "M & DR" pressed into them. The Malton & Driffield Railway was an independent line which opened on 19th May 1853. It climbed over the Wolds with gradients between 1 in 64 and 1 in 104. A.M.*Ross*

G5 67248 pulls its train back off the Driffield line at Malton (Scarborough Road) onto the Scarborough line about 1955. The train had worked from the north via the line from Pilmoor on the east coast main line through Gilling. It was necessary for all trains heading to and from Scarborough on this route to go through the reversal procedure seen in the photograph. The train engine is obscured by the bushes at the far end of the line of coaches. A.L.Brown

B1 61087 storms past Menthorpe gate box on the Selby to Market Weighton line with a summer Saturday extra. This line was built by George Hudson's York & North Midland Railway and was opened on 1st August 1848 having cost £156,000. J.F.Sedgwick

Market Weighton station looking east from the footbridge with Class D49/1 No.62710 LINCOLNSHIRE entering with a westbound train at some time in the 1950s. The high vantage point shows clearly the station walls which formerly supported the overall roof, a feature possessed by this and other country-town stations on the North Eastern. The former engine shed stands on the left of the picture whilst the goods shed is beyond the station to the right of the rear of the train. J.F.Sedgwick.

Market Weighton station and West signal box on 22nd February 1950. The station, like so many others in this part of Yorkshire, originally had an overall roof but the LNER saw fit to dismantle it and BR replaced it with the simple canopies seen here. Until 1865 Market Weighton was the terminus of the lines from York (opened 1847) and Selby (opened 1848) but in that year the eastwards extension to Beverley opened and Market Weighton became a through station. The footbridge, level crossing gates and signal box are pure North Eastern except that the signal box has new concrete steps in place of the original wooden stairs. Notice the upturned plank of wood against the end wall, just above the steps; the plank, when laid down, enabled the signalmen to clean the windows whilst holding on to the handrail and shuffling around the three glazed sides of the box. It was most important that the windows were clean even at the expense of breaking one's neck in the process. W.*Hudson collection.*

22nd February 1950 and still at the west end of Market Weighton station, we have a close-up view of the typical North Eastern signal controlling the junction to Selby and York. The footbridge is a marvellous example of nineteenth century ironwork. The watertank building, which appears to have lost the arch of its original window, is otherwise NER. Besides supplying water to the station and the platform water cranes, this tank also supplied the engine shed until that closed in 1917. W.*Hudson collection.*

Class K1 2-6-0 No.62007 leaves Market Weighton with a train from York to Bridlington. Note the three sets of rails at the side of the tracks, adjacent to the front of the locomotive. These enabled the platelayer gangs to run their working trolleys onto the main line. The locomotive was allocated to Darlington shed and had been borrowed by York shed to work this train. Market Weighton was known as the "Crossroads of the Wolds" as lines went off in four different directions from the station. The tracks on the left form the line to Beverley. A.M.Ross

B1 61276 leaves Market Weighton with a summer weekend extra for the Yorkshire coast resorts. On the left can be seen the open extension of the Y&NMR goods warehouse. The roof was a continuation of that on the main brick building and, when the extension was demolished, as at Filey, it left a building which had a roof with one gable and one hip end. Evidence of engine exhaust blast damage can be seen on the end of the extension. There is a marked contrast between the signals on the right of the train; the very tall upper quadrant lattice post signal was for easy sighting for trains approaching the station around the curve from Driffield and the typical NER slotted timber post bracket signal had a short main support post to make its height more suitable for sighting from the station. A.M.Ross

D49/2 62756 THE BROCKLESBY blasts through Carnaby station just south of Bridlington with a stopping train from Scarborough to Hull during a bright winter's day in the mid 1950s. Gresley's large 4-4-0s, both "Shires" and "Hunts", were the most common engines used on this line after the war up to the introduction of diesel multiple units in the late fifties. 62756 was allocated to Neville Hill shed. A.M.*Ross*

B16s galore at the southern end of Bridlington station. A B16/1 in the background is obscured by B16/2 No.61421 which is double-heading B16/3 no.61467 on a Bridlington - Castleford return excursion. The load of 12 bogies probably justified the assistant engine for the climb over the Wolds. Designed by Sir Vincent Raven as NER class S3, the B16's were used throughout Yorkshire on all types of traffic from slow goods to express passenger. In 1937, No.2364 was rebuilt by Gresley and incorporated his system of Walschaerts valve gear for the outside cylinders and derived motion for the inside cylinder. Six more engines were also rebuilt and given the classification B16/2. In 1944 further rebuilds were authorised by Thompson but this time with three separate sets of Walschaerts valve gear. Seventeen engines received this treatment and became class B16/3. The train is passing under one of the two magnificent NER signal gantries which were adjacent to Bridlington South signal box; the box is just off the left hand side of the photograph. A.M.*Ross*.

A venerable pair of ex-NER 4-4-0s of class D20, No.62395 and its unidentified sister, leave the south end of Bridlington station with the 11.25 a.m. Scarborough (Londesborough Road) to Liverpool (Exchange)in August 1955. The D20s (LNER classification) were the NER class R, designed by Wilson Worsdell and introduced in August 1899 for use on express passenger trains on the east coast main line north of York. Above the second engine can be seen the extension to the original Y&NMR train shed roof which was built in a different style. On the left the support wall for the coal cells can be seen plus a slotted timber post bracket signal. On the right is an ex-NER gas tank wagon. J.W.Armstrong

All the Big Four railway companies had substantial numbers of the versatile 0-6-0 tender locomotive and, during the 1950s, notwithstanding that most of their work was rather mundane and unglamorous, they were often called on at week-ends to work main-line passenger trains. Helping out with a summer Saturday express passenger working and having already conquered the 3½ miles at 1 in 95/100 from Market Weighton up to Enthorpe, valiant J11 No.64286 faces almost 5 miles of 1 in 92 on leaving Bridlington with the 10.30 a.m. Sheffield (Victoria) - Filey Holiday Camp in late August 1953. A.M.Ross.

Scarborough shed's one and only B16, 61445, climbs the 1 in 92 bank from Bridlington to Speeton just north of Flamborough station with the summer Saturdays only 9.52 a.m. Gloucester to Filey holiday camp. This train ran via the Midland "Old Road" between Tapton Junction and Rotherham Masborough. The B16 had taken over from an LMR engine at Masborough Station South, having worked out there earlier in the day with a Leicester train from Scarborough and then going on shed at Canklow. The section of line from Bridlington to Filey was opened one year after that from Seamer to Filey. The delay was caused by difficulties in cutting through the chalk across Flamborough Head, some of which can be seen in the photograph. The first four coaches of the train are ex-LMS vehicles and comprise: Stanier brake third, Stanier third open, Stanier corridor third and another Stanier design of unidentifiable type. A.M.Ross

The north end of Filey station in the mid-1950s with D49/2 No.62751 THE ALBRIGHTON awaiting departure with a Hull to Scarborough train. A number of "Hunts" and "Shires" had their original LNER group standard tenders replaced by GCR and NER types and 62751 is seen coupled to a NER tender. The water crane is of the type introduced by the NER in 1862 and has the spherical style of balance weight. According to railway staff who were employed at the station during the 1950s, when the water crane was removed it was broken into small pieces on site. This debris was then put into the drain under the site of the water crane where, presumably, it remains to this day. The roof had the hip end, seen in the photograph, removed in the late 1960s. The opposite end suffered the same fate a few years later. In 1988 British Rail proposed that the entire roof should be removed but the Minister for the Environment refused permission after considerable objections from various interested parties. Since that time, supported by a considerable financial commitment by the local authorities and English Heritage, British Rail has completed a superb job of restoring the roof to its original appearance. The result of this work is that Filey now has a unique station building as it is the only working example of a G.T.Andrews country station trainshed to retain the original roof style. J.E.Farline collection.

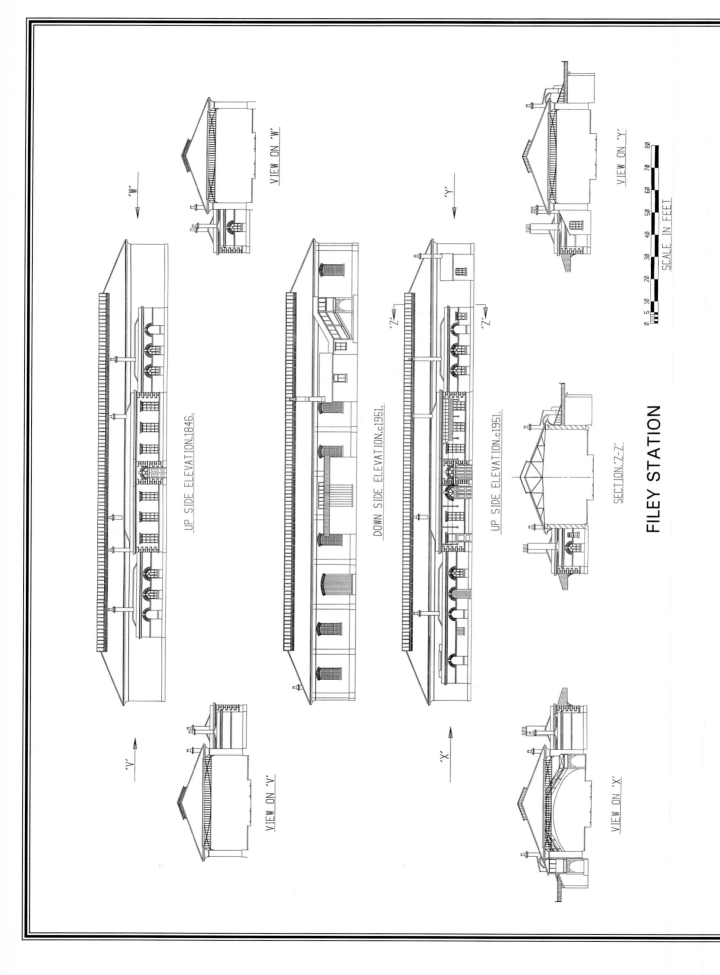

VIEW ON 'W'

VIEW ON 'Y'

'W'

'Y'

UP SIDE ELEVATION.1846.

DOWN SIDE ELEVATION.c.1951.

UP SIDE ELEVATION.c.1951.

'Z'

'Z'

'V'

'X'

VIEW ON 'V'

VIEW ON 'X'

SECTION.'Z-Z'

FILEY STATION

SCALE IN FEET

0 5 10   20   30   40   50   60   70   80

Towards the end of British Railways steam and into the 1970s and 80s, LNER locomotives made a come-back on the Hull to Scarborough line in the shape of the preserved Gresley Pacifics. In this view 4468 MALLARD passes through the train shed at Filey towards Bridlington with one of the special runs in 1988 which celebrated the 50th Anniversary of the locomotive's world speed record. The well maintained footbridge is the standard NER design and is probably unique as the staircase to the down side platform is on the outside of the train shed wall. This staircase is covered by a timber and glass housing to protect passengers from the weather. J.E.Farline

62720 CAMBRIDGESHIRE awaits departure from Seamer with a stopping train from Scarborough (Central) to Hull about 1952. The train formation was typical of those seen on local services up to the mid-1950s and, the fourth carriage, an NER clerestory, still had gas lighting. Seen just above the tender and first coach, is a standard North Eastern footbridge; that and the platform on the left, to which it gave access, were erected in 1911 for the use of passengers requiring the Pickering branch trains. The cattle dock, seen on the right, was put to good use when the weekly agricultural market took place. A pair of horse boxes can be seen in front of the two signalboxes of which that on the right was probably installed in the 1870s when the block system was introduced on the NER. It became a storage cabin after the standard Southern division box was erected in 1911. W.A.Camwell

Filthy B16/1 61422, of York shed, leans into the curve as it takes the Hull line at Seamer Junction with the 11.25 a.m. 'Saturdays only' Scarborough (Londesborough Road) - Liverpool (Exchange) in the late 1950s. This junction was the starting point for the Y&NMR's Seamer to Bridlington branch which was opened as far as Filey on 5th October 1846. It took another year before the remainder of the line was opened. In the background is Seamer West signalbox and the tracks running in from the left are those of the York to Scarborough line. Just off the picture to the left was the junction with the line to Pickering which closed in 1950. J.F.Sedgwick

The approach to the station at Filey Holiday Camp. On the left is the Camp signal box, one of three which were sited at each corner of the triangle of tracks which came off the Filey to Bridlington line between Royal Oak and Hunmanby. All the signal boxes were built to the same LNER type 15 design. The station, which was officially opened on 10th May 1947, had two 900 feet long platforms so that four trains could be handled at the same time. The short branch and station closed in September 1977. A.M.*Ross*.

Class K3 No.61850, of Mexborough (36B) shed, sets out with a train of empty stock from platform 3 at Filey Holiday Camp station in the summer of 1957. The train reporting number, 490, indicates that the engine had arrived earlier with a train from Hull and after uncoupling it would have run round its train to the triangle of lines which formed the Camp branch and the Scarborough - Hull line so that it was facing in the right direction for departure. J.F.*Sedgwick*.

THE NORTH RIDING

BI No.1167, in apple green livery, enters York station in the summer of 1947 with a returning excursion from the east coast and probably bound for the Sheffield area via the S&K Joint line. During the post-war period the BIs were outshopped from their various builders in both green and black liveries with variations of lettering and lining on both colours. 1167 was built by Vulcan Foundry and had black and white lining with numbers and letters painted in yellow unshaded, modified Gill Sans characters 12 inches high. The front bufferbeam number is in the same style and colour but only 6 inches high. There seems to have been some confusion about the train's reporting number. The number chalked on the smokebox door reads 351 SPC and the one attached to the central bufferbeam lamp iron appears to be 215. It is likely that the chalked number was used for a previous working and had not been wiped off. Note the magnificent ex-NER signal gantry in the background. A.L.Brown

B16/1 No.2368, gets into its stride away from York, with a southbound express about 1932. The train is thought to be an excursion returning from Scarborough to Leeds and is running on the Up Leeds line as it passes the platforms at Holgate. The coaches are all ex-NER non-corridor types, predominantly of the high elliptical roof type, introduced from about 1908, but there are four clerestory vehicles towards the rear. Of particular interest, however, is the second coach, a vintage 7 compartment low arc roof design. Perhaps some 40 years old when photographed its white roof indicates that it is ex-works and it may well have lasted into BR ownership. The whole scene is pure NER and only the locomotive livery gives away the fact that the photograph dates from LNER days. W.Hudson collection

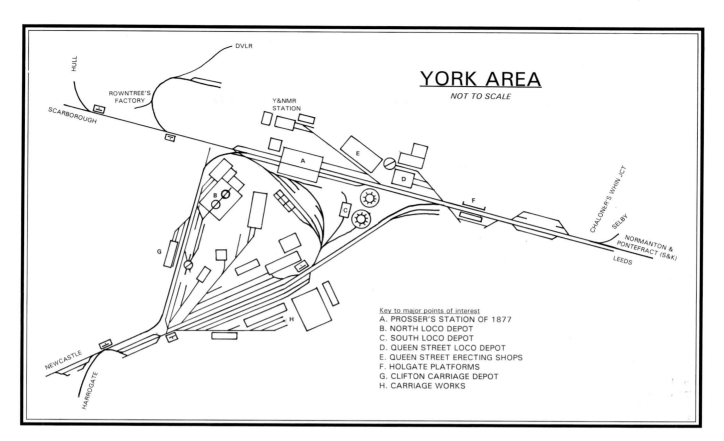

YORK AREA
NOT TO SCALE

DVLR
HULL
ROWNTREE'S FACTORY
SCARBOROUGH
Y&NMR STATION
A
B
C
D
E
F
G
H
CHALONER'S WHIN JCT
SELBY
NORMANTON & PONTEFRACT (S&K)
LEEDS
NEWCASTLE
HARROGATE

Key to major points of interest
A. PROSSER'S STATION OF 1877
B. NORTH LOCO DEPOT
C. SOUTH LOCO DEPOT
D. QUEEN STREET LOCO DEPOT
E. QUEEN STREET ERECTING SHOPS
F. HOLGATE PLATFORMS
G. CLIFTON CARRIAGE DEPOT
H. CARRIAGE WORKS

A combined tractive effort of 56,910 lbs moves a heavy 'summer extra' out of York station in 1955. The leading engine is B16/1 No.61441 of York shed which is assisting an unidentified B1. The train is crossing over to the Scarborough lines and is emerging from the magnificent trainshed designed by the NER architect Thomas Prosser. York station was the climax of Prosser's twenty year term of office with the NER. *C.Boulden.*

No photographic details survive of this picture of Gresley's famous "Hush-hush" locomotive No.10000 (Class W1), but the background, though misty, appears to be York with the river Ouse and the Scarborough branch railway bridge passing over it just behind the locomotive. 10000 is attached to the Dynamometer Car which suggests that testing is taking place and so the date may be early 1930 when a number of tests were being carried out in the area before the 4-6-4 entered revenue-earning service in June of that year. *Authors collection*.

B16/2 No.61455, one of Gresley's rebuilds of Raven's NER class S3 4-6-0, stands at the north end of York station awaiting the arrival of the down SCARBOROUGH FLYER from King's Cross in 1955. The "Flyer" (or "Flier" as it was sometimes written) was a summer only train which, at one time, was the fastest train between King's Cross and York. It was a regular Pacific turn as far as York where engines were changed. Occasionally, for the return Scarborough to York run, Scarborough shed had difficulty in finding suitable power for its only named train even having to resort to using a LMR 4F 0-6-0 on one occasion! *C.Boulden*.

Seen here shortly after Grouping, at the south end of York station, Raven designed class Z Atlantic, 2207 gets away briskly with a Newcastle-Liverpool express. This engine would run as far as Leeds, where it would be exchanged for an LMS western division engine. On some of the cross-Pennine services this engine change took place at York, as witnessed by the presence of an ex LYR Hughes 4-6-0 outside Queen Street shed on the right. The train comprises a wonderful collection of predominantly LNWR passenger stock, but begins with a GNR bogie milk van, behind which are two LNWR 45' 0" arc roof full brakes, the leading one having already received its crimson lake livery. Behind these are an ex-works LNER luggage van and an unidentified short wheelbase vehicle. Next come five LNWR 45'0" arc roof passenger coaches, all still in LNWR livery, while a similarly painted, but more modern elliptical roof brake brings up the rear. To the left of the train the innumerable runs of point rodding, signal wires and other equipment, to operate the complex track layout, necessitates long runs of timber walkways for staff safely. W.H*udson collection*

Even during wartime, improvements were carried out where absolutely necessary. This is the scene at York engine shed about 1943 when wet ash pits were being installed. The disruption this work must have caused would have been tremendous and would have taken the organisation of the depots working to the limits. Locomotives in view are two B16/1s and an A7 freight tank. A*uthors collection*.

B1 61084, of York shed, stands with its train of vans alongside the wooden platform of Rowntrees Halt, York, in September 1950. The halt, which was opened in 1927 under the name Rowntree's Cocoa Works, was situated on a loop off the Foss Islands branch. This was 1 mile 52 chains long and left the Scarborough line a little over a mile from York station, before curving round the eastern outskirts of the city to terminate outside the city walls near Walmgate Bar. Formally opened on 8th December 1879, but not fully operational until 1st January 1880, the line gave rise to much industrial development including the gas and electricity works, Henry Leetham & Sons Ltd (Millers), various coal merchants, the NER laundry and the Derwent Valley Light Railway. Messrs Rowntree's works had its own internal rail system, connected to the branch just south of the halt, and this gave rise to a considerable amount of miscellaneous freight traffic, both in and out, well into the 1980s. The halt itself was used by both staff and parties of visitors to the factory until its closure in the 1980s. W.*Hudson collection*

(*below*) Class V2 No.60964 DURHAM LIGHT INFANTRY has steam to spare as it waits to leave York's platform 16 with a down express in about 1960. The outside platforms at York, added in 1938, present an austere contrast to those under the overall roof. The engine is one of the class which was modified with outside steam pipes in BR days. The leading coach is a Stanier open third, with a second Stanier vehicle behind, and the V2 has almost certainly just taken over a Bristol - Newcastle working. A J72 0-6-0T is standing on the middle road. Note the water crane attached to the underside of the platform awning, and the smoke deflector plates under the footbridge, both features which have long since disappeared from the railway scene.

The vast Permanent Way Engineering yard at York was the home for two of these 15-ton capacity mobile steam cranes purchased by the NER in 1893 from the Leeds crane makers T. Smith & Sons (Rodley) Ltd. Back in the 1890's most railway companies were still purchasing breakdown cranes of this capacity but the North Eastern also equipped its P.W. engineers with them. This 1930's scene shows one of the cranes engaged in the construction of 60ft lengths of track in the yard. The standard garb of the period appears to be the waistcoat and although the crane driver wears an overall jacket, you can bet that underneath will be a waistcoat *Authors coll.*

York Waterworks junction Sunday 12th December 1949. Renewal of the crossings at the north end of the station was taking place and a Cowans Sheldon mobile crane is reversing into position so that a new section of crossing can be swung into place. The crossings enabled trains departing from the westernmost platforms of York station to gain access to the Scarborough line by crossing over the ECML tracks. The Scarborough line is in the background, its junction protected by a nice array of signals on a single gantry. Colour light signals were being introduced at this time and the work seen here was in connection with that project. Closer inspection of the new crossing will reveal a mass of track circuiting wires already in place. The signal box still shows signs of air raid damage from seven years previously and would soon succumb to modernisation. Just below the remains of the original signal box wall, a little boy has a ringside view of the proceedings; no doubt the gentleman by his side was both his father and a railway official. *Authors collection.*

The magnificence of the North Eastern, but in LNER style: Wilson Worsdell's class V 4-4-2 (LNER class C6) No.705 sets off from the south end of York station with an up express on 2nd August 1926. These locomotives were introduced in 1903/4 but No.705 was one of a further batch built in 1910 with slightly larger cylinders and modified splashers and running plate. The LNER gave it a new boiler in 1935. The signals above the engine are interesting as they appear to have a clear lower spectacle. The North Eastern used white lights to denote "clear" up to 1893 when it was recommended that this should be changed to green. It seems strange that clear spectacles should still be in use at York 33 years after this recommendation. It may, of course, be a trick of the light or be caused by the photographic materials available at the time. W.Potter.

Super power near Kirkham Abbey for a 'summer extra' returning from Scarborough to the London Midland Region circa 1958. The locomotives are K3 No.61929 and an unidentified D49/1 4-4-0. The severe curves on this stretch of the Scarborough to York line can be clearly seen. Note the use of bullhead rail on the down line and flat bottom on the up line. J.F.Sedgwick.

An unidentified B1 4-6-0 rushes its train of Scarborough-bound holidaymakers through the delightful setting of Huttons Ambo in the late 1950s. The majority of the coaches are Gresley teak repainted in crimson lake and cream, other vehicles date from the Thompson and BR periods. The train is crossing the bridge over the River Derwent having just passed through Huttons Ambo station. The station building was designed by G.T.Andrews (as were the others on the York to Scarborough line) and built of stone dug from the nearby Hildenley Quarry. The construction of the building was unusual as the stone blocks were held together by their own weight and a series of interlocking grooves and projections. The result was a building with almost invisible joints. The station was closed to passengers on 22nd September and to goods on 10th August 1964. A.M.Ross.

B1 No.61053 of York shed enters Malton station in the summer of 1958, with an express for Scarborough composed of a mixture of Thompson, Gresley and B.R.Mk1 coaches. A North Eastern Railway slotted timber post bracket still survives amongst the predominant B.R. upper quadrants. An unusual feature is the siting of the 40 m.p.h. speed restriction sign which can just be seen hanging from a bracket under the distant signal arm beyond the NER water column. This type of water column was introduced by the North Eastern in 1862. Malton shed (50F) is on the left with an Ivatt Class 2MT 2-6-2T on view. The original NER shed was extended to produce the building seen in the photograph. Note the gas lamp still in use on the platform. A.M.Ross.

Class A8 4-6-2T No.69861 of Malton shed pilots an unidentified B1 past Malton East signal box with a Whitby bound summer 'Saturdays Only' holiday train in 1952. The headcode shows that it is a stopping passenger train which is unusual as this type of train normally carried express code lamps. The train is about to cross the main road to Scarborough and, no doubt, will have created an enormous traffic jam in Malton. (This was before the by-pass was built). In the centre background a NER three doll bracket signal can just be seen. The River Derwent, just visible on the right, was the boundary between the East and North Ridings which meant that, although the market town of Malton was in the North, the station was actually in the East Riding. A.M.Ross.

A8 No.69885, of Scarborough shed, awaits its departure from Scarborough Central. The engine, which would normally be found working on the Scarborough to Whitby line, is in pristine condition and may well have recently been shopped, where it would have received the final BR crest, introduced in 1956. The leading part of the train is a motley collection of coaches, comprising Thompson corridor third E1274E, a Gresley end vestibule third, still in carmine and cream livery and, a Thompson non-corridor brake third. In the left background can be seen the signal box which controlled the station. Built in 1903 this box replaced an earlier timber structure which was cantilevered on all four sides over a narrow brick base, similar to the one at Grosmont. The box seen here was demolished in 1984. R.J.*Buckley*

Incredible as it may seem, this purely North Eastern scene was captured about 15 years after grouping, as D20 (NER class R) 1234 accelerates a train of vintage NER stock past the motive power depot on its way out from Scarborough. At the time the engine still retained its NER smokebox door, chimney and dome. A variety of NER slotted post signals can be seen, but the one in the left foreground is perhaps most interesting, for its lower spectacle plates, which are clearly glazed, should be compared with those at York as discussed earlier. Also worthy of note is the McKenzie & Holland ground signal just in front of the engine's rear driving wheel. The signal gantry over the rear of the train was in use up to 17th May 1970 when it was taken out of use in a resignalling scheme and then demolished. R.J.*Buckley*

A circa 1938 scene at Scarborough shed in LNER days which is almost pure North Eastern Railway in composition. In the foreground are two former East Coast main line greyhounds in the shape of class C6 (NER class V) 4-4-2s, 701 and 704 now reduced to working secondary line duties. On the left is a fine example of a NER gas lamp and, between that and the locomotive, a NER water crane of the type introduced in 1905. Behind the man operating the water crane is one of Gresley's D49 4-4-0s. R.J.Buckley

A line-up of Pacific tank engines in the old NER roundhouse at Scarborough. All these are A8's allocated to Scarborough (50E) and are 69867, 69877 and 69885. The A8's were built by the NER as class D 4-4-4Ts and were introduced in 1913. The first engine to be rebuilt as a class A8 4-6-2T was 2162 which was outshopped in July 1931. It proved to be a success and a rebuilding programme for the other 4-4-4Ts began in January 1933 with the final conversation being made to 1517 in August 1936. The roundhouse was the NER rectangular type and was opened in 1882, replacing a two road shed which had been in existence from the opening of the York to Scarborough line. After the opening of the nearby straight shed the roundhouse was used for storing locomotives and, occasionally, for repairing them. The 44' 8" diameter turntable barred most tender engines from using the roundhouse. J.Bateman collection.

A8 No.69881 and D49/1 No.62731 SELKIRKSHIRE leave Gallows Close Yard in Scarborough with a Railway Correspondence & Travel Society railtour heading for Whitby on 23rd June 1957. Gallows Close was originally intended as the site for the southern terminus station of the Scarborough & Whitby Railway Company but this was rendered unnecessary when the NER agreed to provide accommodation at Central Station. R.J.Buckley

A delightful scene in August 1938 at Levisham on the now preserved Pickering to Grosmont line, as G5 0-4-4T 1886 prepares to leave with a Malton to Whitby stopping train. The station nameboard appears to be the original NER type of enamel plate, with cream letters on a chocolate background. Quite unlike the well known shade used by the GWR, the North Eastern chocolate was a warm reddish-brown colour. W.Potter

Grosmont Junction and station, in the mid 1950s, with the unusual design of NER signal box prominent in the centre. The box was constructed from wood and brick in a similar manner to other Southern division boxes but with the cabin overhanging the base on all four sides. In 1979 it was moved to a new site by the North York Moors Railway Trust. The main station buildings were erected adjacent to the Pickering line on the left and it is these which now form the northern terminus of the North York Moors Railway. The line to the right is the Esk Valley route to Middlesborough. Note the very long check rails required on the tight curve. In the right background is a water tower with an adjacent water crane of typical NER design. R.J.*Buckley*.

Battersby, on the Esk valley line, was one of those isolated rural stations opened simply because there was a junction. Beyond the signal box was Battersby North Junction, where the line to Middlesbrough branched left from the line to Whitby. At the opposite end of the station was Battersby South Junction where the mineral railway to Rosedale branched in a generally southerly direction from the line to Picton, on the ECML. The former route closed entirely in 1928, while that to Picton lost its passenger services in June 1954. In this view, from the station footbridge, in the mid 1950s, the 7.57 a.m. to Whitby sets off in a cloud of steam, while the 6.49 a.m. Whitby to Middlesbrough train stands at the adjacent platform. The train engine is standing somewhere behind the cameraman waiting to complete its run-round movement once the Whitby train has gone. The driver of this engine has been very quick off the mark, as has the guard in changing the tail lamp, for if running to time the Middlesborough train has only been at the platform two minutes. R.J.*Buckley*

B1 61038 BLACKTAIL drifts through Sleights station with the 2.10 p.m. stopping train from Whitby Town to Leeds. Situated in the beautiful valley of the River Esk, which runs just behind the trees on the left, Sleights is approximately mid-way between Whitby and Grosmont. Seen here from the Pickering - Whitby road, the view is full of interesting details, particularly to the modeller. In the background is the small, brick-built NER signal box, close to which is a pedestrian girder bridge over the river. Just in front of this is the yard weigh office which is tilted precariously towards the river. The GNR six wheel non-corridor third in the foreground is being used as a tool van by the Permanent Way department, who also have use of the low sided wagon with its group of cans and drums. The primitive coal staithes, built from sacks of coal are of interest, but even more so are the full sacks of coal in the adjacent open wagon. There are also empty sacks draped over the wagon sides, and some by the coal on the ground. As far as the authors are aware pre-bagged coal was never carried from the colliery by rail. One possibility is that the coal has been acquired from another merchant who had excess stocks, or it could be going out under similar circumstances. More likely it was being delivered to signal boxes and stations along the line. *A.M.Ross*

Class A8 No.9881, leaves the south end of the Esk viaduct with a Whitby - Scarborough stopping train of non-corridor stock which comprises two ex NER vehicles, followed by an LNER built Gresley third, and a GNR brake third. The Esk viaduct was the major engineering feature of the Scarborough to Whitby line and was 915 feet long, with a height from river bed to parapet of 125 feet. The average span of the thirteen arches was 60 feet, with the central one over the river being 64 feet. Work on the viaduct began on 17th October 1882 and was completed in October 1884, at an approximate cost of £40,000. The first train to use the structure passed over on the 24th of that month. It is fortuitous that the well known Whitby photographer, Frank M. Sutcliffe, was active at that time and there exists today an invaluable photographic record of the construction of the viaduct. The locomotive in this view became a 'film star' just after World War II, when it was used to haul a train in the feature film *Holiday Camp*. The film was made on location at Butlin's camp, Filey, but it was decided that the newly built Camp station was not sufficiently attractive. The station seen in the film was that at Sandsend, just north of Whitby, and number 9881 was specially cleaned up for its starring role in the opening scenes.

23rd June 1957 and the RCTS tour again. 69881, which had earlier double-headed 62731 SELKIRKSHIRE from Scarborough, has run round the train at Whitby West Cliff Station. The tank engine is now at the head of the train for the reversal down to Prospect Hill Junction and then on to Whitby Town. Note the signalling of the station for bi-directional operation. The line straight ahead (just look at that gradient) is to Middlesborough via Redcar along the coast. A variation on the standard NER cast iron footbridge connects the platforms. R.J.Buckley.

Whitby Town Station was built by George Hudson's York & North Midland Railway which had purchased the Whitby & Pickering Railway in June 1845. The station was, of course, designed by the Y&NMR's architect George Townsend Andrews of York. At the time of this mid 1950s photograph the train shed had lost its overall roof which was typical of so many of Andrew's station designs. Class A8 4-6-2T 69854 awaits its departure with the 5.35 p.m. stopping train to Battersby. On the left, B.R. Standard class 4MT 2-6-4T 80119 prepares to leave with the 4.20 p.m. to Scarborough. R.J.Buckley.

The bleakness of the northern section of the Yorkshire coastal route is captured in this view as class G5, No.7349 crosses the viaduct over Newholm Beck, between Sandsend and Whitby, with a southbound stopping train. In the background stands the headland of Sandsend Ness, while to the left can be seen the Whitby to Sandsend road. The tubular iron viaduct is one of five similar structures built to carry the line over the valleys which ran down to the sea between Redcar and Whitby. The train of ex NER non-corridor stock consists of brake third, composite, brake third, and apart from the locomotive livery the whole scene could be in pre-grouping days, although it was captured in 1947. W.Hudson *collection*

With the North Sea in the background, A8 class 9881, hauls a northbound stopping train along the cliff side above what is thought to be Sandsend, on a sunny afternoon in the late 1940s. The train consists of an ex NER 10 ton fish van, a Gresley non-corridor brake third and four ex NER non-corridor coaches. The A8's were regular performers on the sinuous, hilly coast line between Scarborough and Whitby, the former being the home of 9881 for many years before withdrawal in June 1958. W.Hudson *collection*

The Whitby to Middlesbrough coastal line was almost as desolate as routes traversing the Pennines and is typified here in this view of Kettleness station, on 18th April 1958. Construction of the line was begun by the Whitby, Redcar & Middlesbrough Railway, but the company was soon in difficulties and the NER was asked to take over, which it did under an Act of Parliament of 19th July 1875. In this view class J25 0-6-0 No.65648, complete with buffer beam snowplough, slows down to enable the single line token to be taken. The engine is returning to Whitby after working the three times a week Whitby to Crag Hall pick-up goods. The neat and tidy appearance of the station, with its platform mounted signal box, belies the fact that it had less than a month to survive, for it was closed entirely on 5th May 1958. A.M.*Ross*

As it followed the coast it was only natural that the Middlesborough to Whitby line should encounter many valleys, five of which were deep enough to require viaducts. Of these the largest was Staithes viaduct, 152 ft high above the Roxby Beck. It had six 60 ft long spans and eleven 30 ft long. Although completed four years before the Tay Bridge disaster of December 1879, the viaduct had not been brought into use and as a consequence of the Scottish tragedy, extensive cross-bracing was added. It also carried a wind gauge and whenever wind pressure reached 28 lb per sq.ft it caused a bell to ring in Staithes signal box. All traffic was then stopped until the wind eased. In this circa 1957 view, one of Thompson's class L1 2-6-4Ts, No.67754, travels south towards Whitby with a stopping passenger train, composed of a Thompson non-corridor brake composite, three ex NER non-corridor thirds and a Thompson brake third. A.L.*Brown*

Before World War Two, Harrogate enjoyed a comprehensive train service over the seven routes radiating from the town. These included long distance services such as Liverpool - Newcastle, and the prestige Pullman services to the capital. Local services ran to Leeds, Bradford, Pateley Bridge, Ripon, Pilmoor, York and Church Fenton. By the mid 1950s however, closures and rationalisation had bitten deeply and local services were primarily those to Leeds and York. In this view N1 0-6-2T 69484 stands at the northbound main line platform at Harrogate with a train from Leeds Central. These engines were rare visitors to the town and as far as the authors are aware the first recorded working of an N1 to Harrogate was during the 1955 ASLEF strike, when a skeleton service was operated by NUR union members. However very careful scrutiny of the original photograph shows the shed plate to be 56B, the number allocated to Ardsley following the regional boundary changes at the end of 1956. Thus the view falls between January 1957 and early 1959, when 69484 was withdrawn. At this time LNER, and pre-group coaching stock, was still much in evidence, but it was showing its age. The Gresley 6-compartment brake third, seen behind the engine, has had the side sheeting of the two compartments next to the brake end repaired by a metal plate, a common practice at the time. Also worthy of note to the modeller is the support post and bracing wires to the water column, which spans two tracks. N.E.*Stead.*

Seen here in 1959 the concourse to platform 5 is full of nostalgic atmosphere and detail, prominent among which is the ironwork carrying the roof. In the foreground the circulating area has a minimum number of columns and the larger spans necessitate deep H-section girders, carried on slender columns, with fluted tops and simple, yet elegant cast iron brackets. From the main girder, lightweight transverse girders, each as a series of circles, run out to support the platform awning. These girders are again supported on lightweight columns, without fluted tops, but a more substantial twin bracket. Below this ironwork the station was always well kept and during the 1920s and 30s it was well known for its floral displays, entirely in keeping with the environment of the town as a whole. An added factor in this caring attitude was that the station was frequented by members of the royal family travelling to and from Harewood House, a few miles to the south of the town. Other details worthy of note include the cast iron platform fencing and the neat, wooden, ticket collectors office, the pillar box with two stamp issuing machines attached and the line of posters proclaiming the delights of York, Whitley Bay, Deal, Thornton Clevelys, Portsmouth & Southsea and Clacton-on-Sea. Almost lost in this sea of detail is the class J39 0-6-0 passing through on the down through road with an ex-NER clerestory roof coach, which is probably an engineers inspection saloon. Finally one might wonder, over 30 years on, if John Farrah is still making his Harrogate Toffee. W.H*udson collection*

The first station in Harrogate was known as Brunswick and was opened in July 1848 as the terminus of the York & North Midland branch from Church Fenton and Wetherby. However passenger traffic on this branch was never significant for Harrogate's affinities lay with Leeds. Connections between the two came a little nearer some twelve months later when the Leeds & Thirsk Railway opened, but this line was barred from entry to Harrogate by Almscliff bank and followed the much easier route through the Crimple valley to Starbeck. Following the formation of the NER in 1854 the matter was looked at again and in August 1859 an Act was obtained sanctioning, inter alia, a new centrally situated station and a link from just north of Pannal, on the L&T line, to a point south of Crimple viaduct on the Y&NM branch. This link and the new station were opened on 1st August 1862, together with a northern link which took through trains back on to the L&T at Bilton Road Junction. Harrogate, now very much a resort and dormitory town for Leeds, Bradford and York, owes its existence to the mineral springs discovered around the end of the sixteenth century. By the mid Nineteenth century it had become highly fashionable among the more wealthy sections of society to 'take the waters' and this must have been at the forefront of Thomas Prosser's mind when he designed what must be accepted as a quite lavish station for a town the size of Harrogate. What is puzzling is why it was felt necessary to provide quadruple tracks through the station when virtually every passenger train stopped there and most freight traffic was routed via Starbeck. The size of the station can be gauged from this view in March 1959 looking south from platform 4 across to No.5, and the bay platforms 6 and 7. Of particular note is the double-sided catch point on the down through road. In the event of a runaway, this would allow the signalman to assess the position of any passenger trains standing in the station, and then divert the offending vehicles accordingly. Having said that there must have been compelling reasons for installing the catch points within station limits in the first place. Another unusual feature is the home signal for the down through road which is mounted on a horizontal bar extending out from the platform building and guyed to the platform canopy. A little to the right is another unusual signal, this time underslung from a vertical post attached to the canopy ironworks. As one would have expected platform 5 to be the main up platform the siting of this signal can only be a very early example of today's common signalling for bi-directional running. *W.Hudson collection*

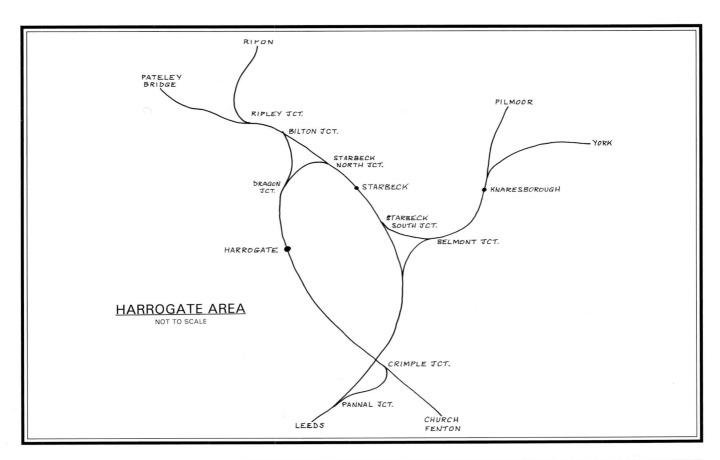

HARROGATE AREA
NOT TO SCALE

RIPON

PATELEY
BRIDGE

RIPLEY JCT.

BILTON JCT.

STARBECK
NORTH JCT.

DRAGON
JCT.

STARBECK

PILMOOR

YORK

KNARESBOROUGH

STARBECK
SOUTH JCT.

BELMONT JCT.

HARROGATE

CRIMPLE JCT.

PANNAL JCT.

LEEDS

CHURCH
FENTON

Edward Thompson's rebuild of Gresley's class D49 4-4-0, No.62768, THE MORPETH, and its crew, pose for the camera at Harrogate station about 1950. As LNER 365, the engine was modified in 1942 from a 3-cylinder engine to one with two inside cylinders, these being the same design as those fitted to the GCR 'Directors'. The engine was given the class designation D under Thompson's standardisation plan for the LNER. The modifications resulted in a reduction of tractive effort from 21,556 lbs to 19,890 lbs and a reduction in weight of $2\frac{1}{2}$ tons. Unfortunately, as with Thompson's redesign of other Gresley locomotives, the modified form did not perform as well as the original. It ended its life at Starbeck shed in October 1952 after being involved in a collision during a shunting movement. The front end of the engine was so severely damaged that Darlington Works decided to cut up the engine. W.Hudson collection.

A3 60036 COLOMBO passes Dragon junction, just north of Harrogate, with a southbound Newcastle to Liverpool express. The train is running on the line from Northallerton. To the right, behind the signalbox, is the line to Starbeck, Knaresborough and York. Note the substantial cottages on the right which were built for the use of railway employees. J.W.*Armstrong*

Most local trains between Leeds and Harrogate followed the old Leeds Northern line via Bramhope tunnel and Arthington, but until its closure in 1964 a few trains followed the hilly route through Crossgates and Wetherby. For most of the post-war years these trains were in the hands of Starbeck's stud of 'Hunt' class D49/2 4-4-0s, as typified by this view of 62765 THE GOATHLAND, with a Leeds bound service at Wetherby, in the mid 1950s. The train is made up of a neat set of NER five compartment brake third, lavatory composite and a second brake third. The lines converging on Wetherby, from Leeds, Harrogate and Church Fenton were all closed to passenger traffic on 6th January 1964, but as late as the early 1960s the Leeds-Wetherby route was graced by regular Liverpool - Newcastle expresses, which served Harrogate without the need to reverse at Leeds City. W.A.*Camwell*

Class G5 0-4-4T 67253 stands at the picturesque station of Dacre with a down train on the Ripley Junction to Pateley Bridge branch. The branch was opened in 1862, at which time Thomas Prosser was the company architect. Perhaps most widely known for his major works, such as York, he also introduced a simple, rustic design for country stations, featuring bold crow step gables. In addition to the Pateley Bridge branch, this design was found on the Esk Valley line and the Lanchester Valley, in County Durham. 67253 worked the branch for almost 33 years, being fitted with push-pull apparatus in 1939. After withdrawal of passenger services on 2nd April 1951 the engine was transferred to the East Riding and was withdrawn from Hull Botanic Gardens in 1958/59. B.G.*Tweed*.

The terminus of the branch was at Pateley Bridge, some 14¹/₂ miles from Harrogate, seen here about 1950, with the single coach branch passenger train, which made four or five return journeys daily. The locomotive, class G5, No.67284, of Starbeck shed, still carries the early livery of BRITISH RAILWAYS, applied up to the adoption of the lion-over-wheel totem in 1949, but the 6-compartment brake third still carries its NER number 2418. The G5 met an earlier fate than its sister engine in the previous plate, being withdrawn from Darlington toward the end of 1956. Rail transport continued a further 6 miles up the valley in the shape of the Nidd Valley Light Railway, opened on 11th September 1907, from its own station in Pateley Bridge to Lofthouse-in-Nidderdale. Opened to facilitate the construction of reservoirs by Bradford Corporation, this line carried a limited passenger service, but was closed entirely on 1st January 1930, when it was no longer required for the carriage of men and building materials. W.A.*Camwell*

D49/2 No.62755 THE BILSDALE, of Starbeck shed, heads north past Wormald Green signal box, south of Ripon, with a down express about 1955. The station buildings can just be seen on the left, while the trailing turnout in the left foreground gave access to the goods yard. The slotted post signal seen above the engine is the Down starter, sited to protect the level crossing. The one above the third coach is the inner home, the two combining to give a very short section, virtually no longer than the station platforms. The leading coach is a North Eastern corridor brake third, while the remainder of the train comprises a mixture of Gresley and Thompson vehicles. J.Bateman collection

B16/1 No.61428 sets off from Ripon with a northbound relief train from Leeds in the mid 1950s. Above the fourth coach can just be seen a rather unusual water crane which was attached to the platform awning and had a pulley system to enable it to be swung out as required. Ripon was the terminus for trains on the Masham branch, but the most frequent service was that provided by the Leeds - Northallerton trains. However judging by the length of the train seen here, it is a longer distance working and may well be a Leeds to Newcastle relief. The leading coach in the train is a Gresley GNR brake composite, behind which is a Gresley corridor composite, then a Thompson corridor first, followed by a Gresley corridor third. Behind these are three more Thompson and two Gresley coaches. Like that at Wormald Green, the signal box is a standard NER type S4 box, introduced in 1905. J.E.Farline collection

J39/1 0-6-0 No.64861, of Starbeck shed, comes off the Masham branch with a through freight train. Although one would expect the train to be running under class K headlamps (pick-up or branch freight), no doubt by the time it had taken up stock at Ripon and stations to Harrogate it would indeed be a through freight train. While the leading low sided wagon must have carried a special load, the covered van for merchandise and the 16 ton all-steel mineral wagon for coal were all that would be required for a two station branch line as BR lost interest in pick-up freight traffic in the late 1950s/early 1960s. The train is running down the rear of the main line platform at Melmerby, where the double sided nameboard would remind passengers that they were approaching the branch platform. The passenger service to Masham was withdrawn as early as 1st January 1931, but goods traffic lingered on until the line was closed completely on 11th November 1963. J.*Bateman collection*

J25 65693 leaves the yard at Thirsk with a down train of empties in 1951. The second wagon of its train is a pre-1923 12 ton private owner, still fitted with grease axleboxes, and carrying the remnants of Firbeck colliery livery. The lines curving away to the right go to Melmerby and the junction with the line from Northallerton to Ripon and Harrogate. The line to Melmerby was closed in 1959. In 1905 the NER brought into use, between Thirsk and Alne, a number of American-style automatic semaphore signals, which were installed by the Hall Automatic Signal Co. of New York. These signals, which were operated by compressed carbon dioxide gas stored in cylinders at the base of each post, gave good service until they were replaced by colour light signals in 1933. The latter can be seen, on the main line, just behind the second and fourth wagons. Note the standard NER cast iron panel water tank on top of a stone base. In the right background is the closed engine shed which had housed its last engines (a pair of J25's) in November 1930; still intact and complete with doors in this view, the shed was finally demolished in 1965. 65693 remained in the Northallerton area until it was transferred to Hull (Dairycoates) in January 1957, from where it was withdrawn in April 1962. *Locofotos.*

An engine from Colwick shed (38A) is a long way from home as it heads northwards through Thirsk station on the East Coast main line in the mid 1950s with a varied collection of mineral wagons in tow. The locomotive is class K2/2 2-6-0 No.61753 and displays its home depot on the LMS/BR-type smokebox door shedplate and also, LNER style, on the buffer beam. J.E.*Farline collection.*

Its early 1950s and G5 0-4-4T 67289 awaits departure time at Boroughbridge on the branch line from Knaresborough to Pilmoor on the East Coast main line. This line was built as two separate branches. Pilmoor to Boroughbridge was opened on 17th June 1847 and Knaresborough to Boroughbridge on 1st April 1875. Note that the station nameboard reads "Borough Bridge", and appears to have been painted by hand so it is probably a mistake by the signwriter. Although the engine has received its BR number it still sports the legend LNER on its tanks and has yet to be fitted with a smokebox numberplate. The train comprises a typical branch line set of brake third/composite/brake third. W.A.*Camwell.*

A3 60073 ST GATIEN roars through Pilmoor station with the up 'Tees-Tyne Pullman', on one of those rare occasions when a named train ran without its customary headboard. The rather austere footbridge was erected at the time of widening, as was the new down platform, on the left. The station building follows the same architectural style as the signal box, while the concrete post and tube fencing contrasts sharply with the NER fencing on the up platform. J.F.*Sedgwick*

Class D20 4-4-0 No.62388 stands alongside the platform-mounted signal box at Jervaulx station on the Northallerton to Hawes Junction line in June 1957. The station building has the typical stepped gables found at other locations on North Riding branch lines. However, this was not a standard feature on the Wensleydale branch, for the line was built in three stages and different architectural styles were used. As was often the case the shelter on the opposite platform is a simple wooden structure and the platform is built up using six layers of interlaced sleepers, with an ash or ballast infilling. On top of this is a row of equally spaced cross members, at 90 degrees to the track, above which is a decking again from sleepers. Careful study of the original photograph suggests that this is covered by a bitumen sheet topped with a layer of gravel chippings. The pile of sleepers on the platform which, judging by the weeds growing round them, have been there for some time and would cause apoplexy to today's Health and Safety inspectors. J.W.*Armstrong*

G5 0-4-4T 7309 about to depart from Richmond with a stopping train to Darlington. The station, designed by G.T.Andrews, was built on the opposite side of the River Swale to the town and included in the construction work was a bridge to give access for passengers from the town. To make it more compatible with the local architecture the station building was designed in the gothic style although the other railway buildings, i.e. engine shed, goods warehouse, etc, were to standard designs used elsewhere. Note the very basic method used to block off the line on the left. The pointwork is supported by interlaced sleepers; a typical NER feature. The second coach of the train is a Gresley semi-corridor lavatory composite but the others are all ex-NER. W.A.*Camwell*.

G5 0-4-4T 67273 stands with its train at the single platform at Middleton-In-Teesdale in the mid 1950s. This station was the terminus of a branch line from Barnard Castle in County Durham which was opened on 12th May 1868. Although Middleton-In-Teesdale was in County Durham, the station was built on the opposite bank of the River Tees and was, therefore, in the North Riding of Yorkshire. The station building seen in the photograph replaced the original in 1888/9. On the right is the single road engine shed. This was a sub-shed of Darlington and was in use up to the introduction of diesel multiple units on 16th September 1957. A 45ft diameter turntable was situated just beyond the water tank but by the date of the photograph it had been filled in. Behind the engine is the goods warehouse and beyond that the elevator housing for a tarmacadam plant which had its own private siding. J.W.*Armstrong*.

Whoopie
go British!

Angela Meads

Bookworm of Retford

First published 2010
Bookworm of Retford, 1 Spa Lane, Retford. DN22 6EA

12345678910

Whoopie Pies Go British!

ISBN: 9780955167454

Printed on paper from a controlled managed source.

Designed and printed by Burgess Design and Print, The Beehive, Beehive Street, Retford, DN22 6JE. www.burgessdesignandprint.com

Acknowledgements:

The Team

The following people have given their wholehearted support in so many ways.
Their enthusiasm, patience and expertise make them precious team members.
Paul Meads, Leah Meads, Katie Meads, Paul Jones,
Bob Burgess, Barbara Burgess, Robert Lloyd and Christina Jones.

Photography: Leah Meads
Whoopie Pie-man Drawings: Katie Meads
Talegate Theatre promotional photography by Leah Meads
Design and Printing: Burgess Design and Print, Retford

Contents

Whoopie Pies go British!

The Amish People of Pennsylvania, USA, have been enjoying Whoopie Pies for many years.

These delicious small cakes have recently become very popular in Britain and here is the first Whoopie Pie book with British ingredients and British measurements, so you too can be part of the great Whoopie Pie experience.

Whoopie Pies are fun to make, so all the family can join in. Adults will enjoy the rich, intense flavour of the Chocolate-Cherry- Pie Whoopies, whilst children will love making and decorating the Choco-Bean Whoopies.

Many pages within this book feature a Whoopie-Pie-Man, and his purpose is simply to catch the eye and attention of our youngest bakers, as most of the recipes are manageable by little hands. Children love baking and Whoopie Pies are a wonderful introduction as they only need a few ingredients and no complicated equipment. Preparation time is about 10 minutes; cooking time is less than 10. So, in no time at all, Whoopie Pies are ready to eat.

To emphasise that baking Whoopie Pies is a great deal of fun, friends James Worthington and Danny Mills from the Talegate Theatre, came to my kitchen one day to try their hand at Whoopie Pie-making. Everything started off well until their characters, Dame Dolly and Idle Jack, became over-enthusiastic at the tasting stage! Still, a great deal of fun was had filming and making Whoopie Pies, but even more fun was had eating them!

Whoopie Pies should not be taken too seriously and there is no need for expensive equipment or fiddly piping-bags. Grab a bowl and a spoon and you're on your way!

Basic Equipment

An electric mixer is very useful for larger quantities of mixture, but most of these recipes create small quantities and therefore the following equipment is all that is necessary.

No piping bags have been used in the recipes. Using a spoon saves time and washing up. With a little practice, perfectly round Whoopie Pies can easily be made, but mis-shapes are just as delicious (and more interesting).

You will need

- ✓ Two metal baking sheets
- ✓ Two re-useable baking-sheet liners.
- ✓ A sieve
- ✓ A large mixing bowl
- ✓ A balloon whisk
- ✓ A teaspoon
- ✓ A tablespoon
- ✓ A knife for spreading the fillings
- ✓ A small glass bowl
- ✓ A small pan
- ✓ A measuring jug
- ✓ A spatula is useful for getting all the mixture out of a bowl.

Fillings for your Whoopie Pies

The fillings suggested here are simple and inexpensive because Whoopie Pies should always be easy to make and affordable.

Buttercream, as a filling, is quick and inexpensive but can seem very sweet. A less sweet alternative filling can be made by mixing a quantity of buttercream with a little whipped double cream or a tablespoon of crème fraiche.

Ready-made cake fillings can now be bought in tubs and many are now without artificial flavours or preservatives. These tubs are useful to have in your store cupboard if you make small batches of Whoopie Pies.

Basic buttercream

225g icing sugar
100g soft butter
1 teaspoon vanilla extract (or any other flavour)

Mix all the ingredients in a bowl.

Coffee buttercream

To the above, add 1 or 2 teaspoons of instant coffee mixed with a tablespoon of hot water.

Chocolate

To the vanilla buttercream mixture, add 2 teaspoons of cocoa powder and a teaspoon of milk if required.

Orange, Lemon or Lime

To the vanilla mixture add 2 teaspoons of the freshly squeezed juice. A little grated zest can be added too.

Marshmallow filling

Jars of the spreadable, American marshmallow fluff can now be found in some shops; however, here is an easy and less expensive alternative.
2 tablespoons butter
350g marshmallows
50mls double cream

Heat all the ingredients gently in a pan until they have melted. Allow to cool until the mixture is spreadable.

Dark chocolate ganache

200g dark chocolate
100mls whipped double cream
Melt the chocolate in a small bowl over a pan of water, stir in the cream and mix well.
Leave to cool before spreading.

Make a larger quantity to use as a dipping sauce for whoopie-halves.

Savoury cheese and onion filling

2 tablespoons ricotta cheese
1 tablespoon Philadelphia® cheese spread
1 tablespoon onion relish

Mix all the ingredients together, making more as required.

The above quantities are a suggestion only. Omit the onion relish if you wish and add more cheese spread: for example,
2 tablespoons ricotta cheese
2 tablespoons Philadelphia® cheese spread

Whipped cream fillings

Whipped double cream is ideal for mixing with any mashed fruit such as strawberries, raspberries or ripe bananas. Mash the fruit first, then fold into the whipped cream.

Basic Chocolate

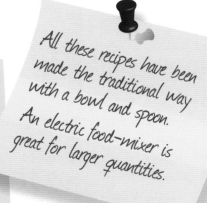

All these recipes have been made the traditional way with a bowl and spoon. An electric food-mixer is great for larger quantities.

Ingredients

50g soft butter
50g brown sugar
1 egg
100g plain flour
1 teaspoon baking powder
1 heaped tablespoon cocoa powder (or 25g)
2 tablespoons milk

Method

Cover 2 baking trays with re-useable baking sheets or baking parchment.
Preheat your oven to 170°/gas mark 4/moderate.
Mix together the soft butter and sugar.
Add the egg and beat well.
Add the flour, baking powder and cocoa powder and 1 tablespoon of milk.
Mix well.
Add another tablespoon of milk if required.
Use a teaspoon to put small amounts of mixture onto the baking trays. Leave a 2-3 cm gap between each whoopie as they will spread.
Cook for 7-8 minutes.
Remove from the oven and allow to cool.
When cool, fill with buttercream (see page 10).

Basic Vanilla

Ingredients

50g caster sugar
50g soft butter
1 egg
1 teaspoon vanilla extract
100g plain flour
1 heaped teaspoon baking powder
1-2 tablespoons of milk

Method

Cover 2 baking trays with re-useable baking sheets or baking parchment.
Preheat your oven to 170°/gas mark 4/moderate.
Mix together the soft butter and sugar.
Add the egg and beat well.
Add the vanilla extract.
Add half the flour plus the baking powder.
Add a tablespoon of milk.
Add the rest of the flour and mix well.
Use a teaspoon to put small amounts of mixture onto the baking trays.
Leave a 2-3 cm gap between each whoopie as they will spread during cooking.
Cook for 7-8 minutes.
Remove from the oven and allow to cool.
When cool, fill with chocolate buttercream (see page 10).

Non-stick baking sheet-liners are a marvellous invention. They are re-usable, economical and wash easily.

Traditional Amish Recipe

ingredients

125g softened butter
150g caster sugar
2 eggs
1 teaspoon vanilla extract
½ teaspoon salt

100mls water
100mls milk
250g flour
1 heaped teaspoon baking powder
3 tablespoons cocoa powder

Method

Cover 2 baking trays with re-useable baking sheets or baking parchment.
Preheat your oven to 170°/gas mark 4/moderate.
Mix together the soft butter and sugar.
Add the eggs and beat well.
Add the vanilla extract and salt.
Add the water and milk and mix well.
Gradually stir in the flour a little at a time.
Add the baking powder.
Add the cocoa and mix well.
Use a teaspoon to put small amounts of mixture onto the baking trays. Leave a 2-3 cm gap between each whoopie as they will spread. Cook for 7-8 minutes. Remove from the oven and allow to cool.
When cool, fill with marshmallow filling (page 11).

Ginger Ninja

Ginger nut biscuits are a great British favourite and these Ginger Ninja Whoopie Pies have quite a flavoursome kick.

ingredients

100g soft butter
100g dark brown sugar
1 large egg
1 tablespoon golden syrup
2-3 teaspoons ginger powder
1 teaspoon cinnamon
200g plain flour
1 heaped teaspoon baking powder
75ml milk

Method

Cover 2 baking trays with re-useable baking sheets or baking parchment.
Preheat your oven to 170°/gas mark 4/moderate.
Mix together the soft butter and sugar.
Add the egg and beat well.
Add the golden syrup and mix well.
Add the ginger and cinnamon and mix well.
Add some of the flour and then some of the milk.
Add the baking powder, the rest of the milk and the rest of the flour.
Mix well.
Use a teaspoon to put small amounts of mixture onto the baking trays. Leave a 2-3 cm gap between each whoopie as they will spread. Cook for 8 minutes. Remove from the oven and allow to cool.
When cool, fill with buttercream (page 10). You could add a teaspoon of ginger to the buttercream for a stronger flavour.

Choca-Mocha

Ingredients

100g soft butter
100g dark brown sugar
1 egg
3 tablespoons cocoa powder
1 tablespoon instant coffee powder

200g plain flour
1 heaped teaspoon baking powder
100mls milk

Method

Cover 2 baking trays with re-useable baking sheets or baking parchment.

Preheat your oven to 170°/gas mark 4/moderate.

Mix together the soft butter and sugar.

Add the egg and beat well.

Add the cocoa powder and the coffee.

Add half the flour and half the milk and mix well.

Add the rest of the flour and baking powder and mix well.

Use a teaspoon to put small amounts of mixture onto the baking trays. Leave a 2-3 cm gap between each whoopie as they will spread. Cook for 8 minutes. Remove from the oven and allow to cool.

When cool, fill with coffee or vanilla buttercream (page 10).

Chocolova

ingredients

100g soft butter
100g dark brown sugar
2 eggs
100g dark chocolate (70% cocoa solids)
2 teaspoons vanilla extract
100mls milk
200g plain flour
1 heaped teaspoon baking powder

This is a chocolatey alternative to the famous Pavlova dessert. Decorate with strawberries, raspberries or blueberries. Crushed meringues can be used if mini-meringues are not available. Pile the large whoopie high and use as little or as much cream as you like.

For the Topping

300ml carton of double cream. Strawberries and (bought) mini-meringues to decorate.

Method

Cover 2 baking trays with re-useable baking sheets or baking parchment.
Preheat your oven to 170°/gas mark 4/moderate.
Place a small glass bowl on top of a small pan filled with water so that the water just touches the bottom of the bowl. Heat the water to simmering point.
Break the chocolate into the bowl, add the butter and sugar and gently melt them; keep stirring.
Allow to cool a little, then add the egg and beat well.
In a larger bowl mix the flour and baking powder, add the melted chocolate mixture and mix well; gradually add the milk and mix well again.
Pour the mixture onto a baking sheet to make one large round shape, gently spreading the mixture until it is about 1cm thick.
Bake for about 12-15 minutes until the top is firm. Allow to cool, and then place the large half-whoopie upside down on a serving plate. When the whoopie base is completely cold, cover with whipped cream, raspberries or strawberries and scatter mini-meringues on top.
Eat the same day.

Hunny Bunny

Winnie the Pooh, a most loveable British bear, first made his appearance in the 1920s. Winnie has always had great trouble with 'wobbly' spellings, but honey, however spelled, will taste as sweet! Here's a great flavoured 'hunny' whoopie to share with Rabbit.

These Whoopie Pies will be fairly flat because of the honey, but the flavour is lovely.

Ingredients

50g light brown sugar
50g soft butter
1 egg
2 dessertspoonfuls honey
100g plain flour
1 teaspoon baking powder

Method

Cover 2 baking trays with re-useable baking sheets or baking parchment.
Preheat your oven to 170°/gas mark 4/moderate.
Mix together the soft butter and sugar.
Add the egg and beat well.
Add the honey and mix well.
Add the flour and the baking powder and mix very well.
Use a teaspoon to put small amounts of mixture onto the baking trays. Leave a 2-3 cm gap between each whoopie as they will spread. Cook or 8 minutes. Remove from the oven and allow to cool.
When cool, take a whoopie-half and drizzle with runny honey.

A Trifle Whoopie

To make one large trifle

6-8 whoopie-halves
1 packet of jelly mix.
A small tin of fruit, drained (chopped, soft,
fresh fruit can be used too)
1 tin custard
Small carton double cream (or whipping cream)
1 teaspoon icing sugar or caster sugar
Sprinkles to decorate

This dessert looks wonderful and hides the fact that you might be using a number of whoopie mis-shapes, or Whoopie Pies that are a day or two old. Freshly baked Whoopie Pies will work well too.

Method

Place the whoopie-halves in the bottom of a serving dish.
Cover the whoopies with the drained fruit.
Make half a pint of jelly (according to the packet instructions) and pour over the fruit. Place the dish in the fridge to allow the jelly to set.
Pour custard on top of the jelly.
Pour the cream into a small dish, add the sugar and whisk until it thickens. Add this to the top of the trifle. Sprinkles can be added on top for that retro party look.

Individual Mini Trifles

Small, individual portions of trifle can be made by making a batch of Whoopie Pies in two sizes.
Use the Basic Vanilla Whoopie Pie recipe on page 16.
Use half the mixture to make 6 – 8 small whoopie-halves on one baking tray and the rest of the mixture to make 6 – 8 larger whoopie-halves by using a dessert spoon instead of a teaspoon.
Allow to cool. Continued . . .

Continued . . .

Place a whoopie-half in the base of each individual serving dish (sundae dish)

Now follow the method for the big trifle (left) until you have completed all stages for each trifle.

Finally, take a small whoopie-half, dip the top surface in a little cream, place it base-side down on the trifle and sprinkle with a few cake decorations.

Choco-Bean

This one pleases adults and children! If you are in a desperate hurry, the Smarties® can be added at the final mixing stage, but children will have fun pushing the chocolate beans into the mixture, making sure each whoopie pie gets a good selection of colours.

Ingredients

50g caster sugar
50g soft butter
1 egg
1 teaspoon vanilla extract

100g plain flour
1 heaped teaspoon baking powder
1-2 tablespoons of milk
Chocolate beans or Smarties®

Method

Cover 2 baking trays with re-useable baking sheets or baking parchment.
Preheat your oven to 170°/gas mark 4/moderate.
Mix together the soft butter and sugar.
Add the egg and beat well.
Add the vanilla extract.
Add half the flour plus the baking powder.
Add a tablespoon of milk.
Add the rest of the flour.
Mix well.
Use a teaspoon to put small amounts of mixture onto the baking trays. Leave a 2-3 cm gap between each whoopie as they will spread. Push 4 or 5 chocolate beans into each whoopie pie.
Cook for 7 minutes. Remove from the oven and allow to cool.
When cool, fill with chocolate buttercream (page 10) or the marshmallow filling, (page 11).

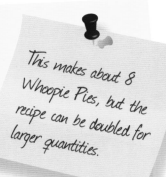

This makes about 8 Whoopie Pies, but the recipe can be doubled for larger quantities.

Chocolate Cherry Pie

Ingredients

100g brown sugar
100g soft butter
2 eggs
8 tablespoons cherries in syrup
200g plain flour
1 ½ heaped teaspoons baking powder

Less is more! Leave over-decorating to the children. Classy, adult Whoopie Pies don't have sprinkles, just lots of flavour.

Filling

Small carton of double cream (whipped) and some left-over cherry juice.

Method

Cover 2 baking trays with re-useable baking sheets or baking parchment.
Preheat your oven to 170°/gas mark 4/moderate.
Mix together the soft butter and sugar.
Add the eggs and beat well.
Add the cherries. If you are using a food processor, the cherries will be automatically cut into fine pieces but if you are hand mixing or using a conventional electric mixer, the cherries will need chopping into small pieces before adding to the mixture.
Add the flour and baking powder and mix well. Another tablespoon or two of cherry syrup may be required to make the mixture the right consistency.
Place 18-20 spoonfuls of mixture on the baking trays.
Cook for 8 minutes. Remove from the oven and allow to cool.
When cool, fill with a mixture of whipped double cream and a tablespoon of cherry juice..

This recipe is one of my favourites for taste and texture. The Whoopie Pies last very well in an airtight container for 2-3 days, but before you try this recipe, I recommend you make the basic chocolate whoopie pie first, so you will know how much extra cherry syrup to add to get the correct consistency.

Coconut

Ingredients

50g soft butter
50g caster sugar
50g desiccated coconut
1 egg
100g plain flour
1 teaspoon baking powder
3-4 tablespoons milk

All these recipes have been made the traditional way with a bowl and spoon. An electric food-mixer is great for larger quantities.

Method

Cover 2 baking trays with re-useable baking sheets or baking parchment.

Preheat your oven to 170°/gas mark 4/moderate.

Mix together the soft butter and sugar.

Add the eggs and beat well.

Add the coconut, the flour, the baking powder and mix well.

Use a teaspoon to put small amounts of mixture onto the baking trays. Leave a 2-3 cm gap between each whoopie as they will spread.

Cook for 7-8 minutes.

Remove from the oven and allow to cool.

When cool, fill with buttercream (page 10).

Cherry Bakewell

ingredients

50g soft butter
50g caster sugar
1 egg
50g ground almonds
100g plain flour
1 teaspoon baking powder
1 teaspoon almond flavouring or vanilla extract
2-3 tablespoons milk

Bakewell tarts and Bakewell puddings are as British as the Derbyshire Hills. These Whoopie Pies are a delicious variation of the Cherry Bakewell.

Method

Cover 2 baking trays with re-useable baking sheets or baking parchment.

Preheat your oven to 170°/gas mark 4/moderate.

Mix together the soft butter and sugar.

Add the eggs and beat well.

Add the vanilla extract or almond flavouring.

Add the ground almonds, flour and baking powder and mix really well.

You may need to add 2-3 tablespoons of milk to create a nice dropping consistency.

Use a teaspoon to put small amounts of mixture onto the baking trays. Leave a 2-3 cm gap between each whoopie as they will spread.

Cook for 7-8 minutes.

Remove from the oven and allow to cool.

When cool, take two halves and fill with vanilla buttercream.

Glacé Icing

100g icing sugar   2 tablespoons water

Mix the icing sugar and the water together. Place a very small amount on top of each whoopie pie; add a cherry on top.

Gluten-Free Chocolate

Ingredients

50g soft butter
50g dark brown sugar
50g cocoa powder
2 eggs
1 teaspoon vanilla essence
100g gluten-free self-raising flour
1 tablespoon milk (if the eggs are small)

Method

Cover 2 baking trays with re-useable baking sheets or baking parchment.
Preheat your oven to 170°/gas mark 4/moderate.
Mix together the soft butter and sugar.
Add the eggs and beat well.
Add the cocoa powder and the flour,
mix well, adding a tablespoon of milk if the mixture seems too dry.
Use a teaspoon to put small amounts of mixture onto the baking trays.
Leave a 2-3 cm gap between each whoopie as they will spread.
Cook for 7-8 minutes.
Remove from the oven and allow to cool.
When cool, take a whoopie-half and spread with a filling of your choice
and place another whoopie-half on top.

Gluten-Free and Dairy-Free Cheesy Flavoured Savouries

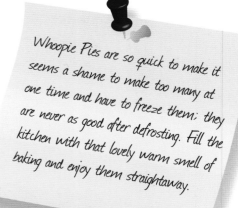

Ingredients

50g dairy-free cheese substitute (available from health food shops that have a chill cabinet)
Pinch of salt
Pinch of garlic powder
1 large tablespoon fruit purée
1 large egg
100g gluten-free self raising flour
3-4 tablespoons water

Whoopie Pies are so quick to make it seems a shame to make too many at one time and have to freeze them; they are never as good after defrosting. Fill the kitchen with that lovely warm smell of baking and enjoy them straightaway.

Method

Cover 2 baking trays with re-useable baking sheets or baking parchment.
Preheat your oven to 170°/gas mark 4/moderate.
Blend all the ingredients together except the flour and water.
Then add the flour and gradually add water one tablespoon at a time. Do not make the mixture too wet.
Place teaspoonfuls of the mixture onto a baking sheet, leaving a 2cm gap in between each heap.
Cook for 7-8 minutes.
Remove from the oven and allow to cool.
When cool, fill with 2-3 tablespoons of dairy-free cheese substitute mixed with a few freshly chopped chives.

Low-Sugar Whoopie

Ingredients

50g Splenda® or other granulated sugar substitute
50g soft butter
1 egg
1 teaspoon vanilla extract
100g plain flour
1 heaped tablespoon baking powder
1-2 tablespoons milk if required

Method

Cover 2 baking trays with re-useable baking sheets or baking parchment.
Preheat your oven to 170°/gas mark 4/moderate.
Blend the butter with the sugar substitute.
Add the egg and beat well.
Add the vanilla extract.
Add the flour and baking powder and mix well. If the mixture seems to dry, add a tablespoon or two of milk.
Use a teaspoon to put small amounts of mixture onto the baking trays. Leave a 2-3 cm gap between each whoopie as they will spread.
Cook for 7-8 minutes.
Remove from the oven and allow to cool.

Filling

To keep the sugar content as low as possible, here are some suggestions.
• Mashed strawberries in whipped double cream
• Low-sugar jam
• A mixture of whipped double cream (small carton) and a tablespoon of low-sugar jam mixed together

Cheesy Savoury

Ingredients

100g soft butter
2 eggs
½ teaspoon salt
1 teaspoon baking powder
½ teaspoon garlic powder or paste
100g Parmesan cheese
200g plain flour

Method

Cover 2 baking trays with re-useable baking sheets or baking parchment.
Preheat your oven to 170°/gas mark 4/moderate.
Mix the butter, eggs and salt, add the garlic powder or paste and the Parmesan cheese; mix well.
Add the baking powder and flour and mix very well.
Use a teaspoon to put small amounts of mixture onto the baking trays. Leave a 2-3 cm gap between each whoopie as they will spread.
Cook for 8-10 minutes.
Remove from the oven and allow to cool.
When cool, fill with a cream cheese filling.
The Whoopie Pie in the photo has a mixed filling of cream cheese and onion relish.

Jam Tart

Ingredients

50g caster sugar
50g soft butter
1 egg
1 teaspoon vanilla extract
100g plain flour
1 heaped teaspoon baking powder
1-2 tablespoons of milk
Jam (any flavour, but strawberry is traditional)
Icing sugar for dusting

The Queen of Hearts she made some tarts all on a summer's day; The Knave of Hearts he stole the tarts and took them clean away. The King of Hearts called for the tarts and beat the Knave full sore The Knave of Hearts brought back the tarts and vowed he'd steal no more.

(18th century poem)

Method

Mix together the soft butter and sugar.
Add the egg and beat well.
Add the vanilla extract.
Add half the flour plus the baking powder.
Add a tablespoon of milk.
Add the rest of the flour and mix well.
Use a teaspoon to put small amounts of mixture onto the baking trays.
Leave a 2-3 cm gap between each whoopie as they will spread. Cook for 7-8 minutes.
Remove from the oven and allow to cool.
Spread half the whoopies with jam. The other whoopies will need a 2cm hole making in the middle of each one. If you haven't got a small cutter, use the neck of an up-turned small water bottle. Push firmly down into the centre of a whoopie-half and remove the piece of cake from the centre. Place the whoopie ring on top of the jam; dust with icing sugar.

Apple Pie

ingredients

50g caster sugar
50g soft butter
1 egg
100g plain flour
1 heaped teaspoon baking powder
1-2 tablespoons of milk
1 dessertspoon fruit purée
This makes 6 medium sized pies.

Pre-heating your oven to the right temperature is very important.

Method

Cover 2 baking trays with re-useable baking sheets or baking parchment.
Preheat your oven to 170°/gas mark 4/moderate.
Mix together the soft butter and sugar.
Add the egg and beat well.
Add the fruit purée.
Add half the flour and baking powder, a tablespoon of milk and mix well.
Add the rest of the flour and a little more milk if necessary; mix well.
Use a dessertspoon to place 12 heaps of mixture onto the baking trays. Leave a 2-3 cm gap between each whoopie as they will spread.
Cook for about 8 minutes.
Remove from the oven and allow to cool. When the Whoopie Pies are cold, fill with spoonfuls of apple purée or chunky apple sauce. Serve with custard or ice-cream.

Whoopie Gateau

Ingredients for 1 large vanilla whoopie

50g caster sugar
50g soft butter
1 eggs
1 teaspoon vanilla extract
100g plain flour
1 heaped teaspoon baking powder
1-2 tablespoons of milk

Ingredients for the 2 large chocolate whoopies

100g soft butter
100g brown sugar
2 eggs
200g plain flour
2 teaspoons baking powder
2 heaped tablespoons cocoa powder
3-4 tablespoons milk

Method for Vanilla Whoopie

Cover a baking tray with a re-useable baking sheet or baking parchment.
Preheat your oven to 170°C/gas mark 4/moderate.
Mix together the soft butter and sugar.
Add the egg and beat well.
Add the vanilla extract.
Add half the flour plus the baking powder.
Add a tablespoon of milk.
Add the rest of the flour and mix well.
Place all the mixture in the centre of one baking tray.
Spread it out a little, to about 1cm thick. Cook for 7-8 minutes, then remove from the oven and allow to cool.

Method for the two Chocolate Whoopies

Cover two baking trays with re-useable baking sheets or baking parchment.
Preheat your oven to 170°C /gas mark 4/moderate.
Mix together the soft butter and sugar.
Add the eggs and beat well.
Add the flour, baking powder and cocoa powder and 2 tablespoons of milk. Mix well.
Add another tablespoon of milk if the mixture seems too thick.
Divide the mixture between two baking trays. Spread the mixture out a little to about 1cm thick. Cook for 8-10 minutes and allow to cool.

This gateau is made from three large whoopies. The combination of whoopie layers is your choice, but the photo shows a slice of gateau made from two chocolate layers and one vanilla layer in the middle.

The Fillings

Assemble this gateau straight onto a serving plate by placing the first chocolate whoopie with the flat side facing upwards.

Assemble the layers with fillings of your choice such as butter cream or fresh cream.
A layer of cherries in syrup can be added to the bottom layer before adding fresh whipped cream.
Add the vanilla layer, followed by more cream (or buttercream) and finally, carefully place the last chocolate layer on top. Dust with icing sugar.
For a very neat finish, use a small plate to cut around each whoopie using a bread-knife. Repeat this with each whoopie and you will then have three layers, matching in size.

Queen Victoria enjoyed a slice of light sponge
cake with a cup of tea in the afternoon.
This Whoopie Pie is also very light and a
perfect partner for a lovely cup of tea.

Victoria Sandwich

ingredients

100g caster sugar
100g soft butter
2 eggs
2 teaspoon vanilla extract
200g plain flour
1 ½ heaped teaspoon baking powder
50mls milk

For the best flavour, use pure vanilla extract and not artificial vanilla essence or flavouring.

For the filling

Small carton of double cream
Jam for spreading

Method

Cover 2 baking trays with re-useable baking sheets or baking parchment.
Preheat your oven to 170°/gas mark 4/moderate.
Mix together the soft butter and sugar.
Add the eggs and beat well.
Add the vanilla extract.
Add half the flour plus the baking powder.
Add the milk gradually, followed by the rest of the flour and mix very well.
Use a teaspoon to put small amounts of mixture onto the baking trays.
Leave a 2-3 cm gap between each whoopie as they will spread.
Cook for 7-8 minutes, then remove from the oven and allow to cool.
Fill with whipped double cream and jam. Dust over the top with icing sugar.

Strawberry Sensations

ingredients

50g caster sugar
50g soft butter
1 egg
1 teaspoon vanilla extract
1 heaped tablespoon of smooth strawberry jam
100g plain flour
1 heaped teaspoon baking powder
1-2 tablespoons of milk

For the filling

Small carton of double cream
Smooth strawberry jam or, when English strawberries are in season, take a handful of ripe strawberries and mash them with a fork before mixing with the cream.

Method

Cover 2 baking trays with re-useable baking sheets or baking parchment.

Preheat your oven to 170°/gas mark 4/moderate.

Mix together the soft butter and sugar.

Add the egg and beat well.

Add the vanilla extract and the jam and mix well.

Add half the flour plus the baking powder.

Add a tablespoon of milk. Add the rest of the flour and mix well.

Use a teaspoon to put small amounts of mixture onto the baking trays. Leave a 2-3 cm gap between each whoopie as they will spread. Cook for 7-8 minutes.

Remove from the oven and allow to cool.

In a bowl whip together the double cream and smooth strawberry jam to make the filling.

Fill the whoopies with the cream and jam mixture.

Lemon Drizzle

Ingredients

50g caster sugar
50g soft butter
1 egg
1 tablespoon of fresh lemon juice plus the zest of 1 lemon
100g plain flour
1 heaped teaspoon baking powder
1-2 tablespoons of milk

Salted or unsalted butter? Whoopie Pies are really not that fussy, so use whichever type you have bought.

Method

Cover 2 baking trays with re-useable baking sheets or baking parchment.
Preheat your oven to 170°/gas mark 4/moderate.
Mix together the soft butter and sugar.
Add the egg and beat well.
Add the zest and lemon juice and mix well.
Add the flour and baking powder and mix really well adding a little more milk if required.
Use a teaspoon to put small amounts of mixture onto the baking trays.
Leave a 2-3 cm gap between each whoopie because they will spread during cooking.
Cook for 7-8 minutes.
Remove from the oven and allow to cool.
When cool, fill two halves with lemon buttercream (see page 11).
Make a small amount of lemon glacé icing by mixing 1 tablespoon of fresh lemon juice with enough icing sugar to make a thick paste. Drizzle a small amount of icing onto each whoopie pie.

A Winter Whoopie

Ingredients

100g caster sugar
100g soft butter
2 eggs
2 teaspoons mixed spice
1 tablespoon apple sauce
A handful of dried fruit such as raisins or sultanas
200g plain flour
1 teaspoon baking powder
2 tablespoons of milk (if required)

A tub of brandy butter for the filling (optional)

Method

Cover 2 baking trays with re-useable baking sheets or baking parchment.
Preheat your oven to 170°/gas mark 4/moderate.
Mix together the soft butter and sugar.
Add the eggs and beat well.
Add the spice and apple sauce and mix well, and then add the dried fruit; mix well again.
Add the flour and baking powder gradually. You may need a little milk at this stage but add it one tablespoon at a time until the mixture is blended and easy to push off a spoon with your finger.
Place small heaps of mixture onto the baking trays; half a dessert spoonful is about the right amount.
Leave a 2-3 cm gap between each whoopie as they will spread.
Cook for 8-10 minutes.
Remove from the oven and allow to cool before filling with brandy butter (or buttercream or even clotted cream).

'Sugar and spice and all things nice';
that's what Winter Whoopies are
made of!

Why not bring a little festive cheer to your Whoopies? Make them a real treat for Christmas.

Make Whoopie Pies in your Microwave and Halogen Oven

Microwave Oven Method – great for making Whoopie Pies in a caravan.

Whoopie Pies cook best in a conventional oven; however, if a microwave oven is the only facility available at the time, it may be useful to know that it is possible to cook the basic vanilla, or chocolate Whoopie Pie mixtures.

Remove the glass plate from your microwave oven and cover it with a piece of re-useable baking sheet. Place small teaspoonfuls of mixture on the sheet and return to the oven. Cook on the medium setting for no more than 50 seconds. Remember, the mixture will continue cooking after it has been taken out of the oven, so it is important not to over-cook.

Have your filling ready straightaway as these whoopies are best eaten whilst very fresh.

Alternatively, dip warm whoopie-halves into warm melted chocolate.

60

Halogen Oven Method

Halogen ovens are capable of cooking in a very similar way to conventional ovens, but they are faster. The powerful heating element in a halogen oven means that most Whoopie Pies will be cooked in about 4 minutes. The appearance of the Whoopie Pies may be slightly different from those cooked in a conventional oven. You may find that the outer surfaces of the Whoopie Pies are a little crisper but the inside will still be light and fluffy.

Use a metal tray covered in a re-useable baking sheet. I use a small pizza tray as it is just the right shape for a halogen oven. Place small amounts of Whoopie Pie mixture onto the baking sheet, using a teaspoon. The mixture needs to be placed around the edge of the baking sheet to hold it down during cooking. The halogen oven has a powerful fan which will otherwise blow the baking sheet about.

On the high rack, cook on 175°C for about 4 minutes or until the base of the Whoopie Pie has set. The tops of the Whoopie Pies will have a slightly toasted appearance.

If you have a small halogen oven, place the baking tray on the rack and cook on 200c for about 5 minutes.

The vanilla flavoured Whoopie Pies will start to go golden before the inside is cooked, but continue cooking as this will not spoil the Whoopie Pie. A crunchy outside and soft insides to your Whoopie Pie is a lovely combination.

chocolate beans

Decoration Ideas

sprinkles galore

62

butterfly

cherries

fairy dust

63

sprinkles

Whoopsies

or out-takes to you and me!

If your baking doesn't always turn out quite as neatly as the lovely Whoopie Pies in the photos, then don't worry, because neither does mine! And just to prove it, here are some of the whoopie photos that didn't make it to the main pages.

These microwave whoopies (above) need 2 more seconds cooking time.

Don't fill whoopee pies if they are still warm because the cream will run!

Odd shapes still taste great.

No Whoopie Pies were harmed during the making of these – and we ate them anyway!

Ooops . . .

Pale and very uninteresting!

Caught licking the spoon!

This demonic bird-like creature caused a stir!

Find out how Idle Jack got chocolate on his face by visiting www.youtube.com